"This is a marvelous book—simple, clear, direct, full of light. What I love about Jon is that he doesn't give us philosophy, metaphysics, or non-dual dogmatism. Instead, he points in plain language to the non-conceptual, embodied experiencing of this moment. He invites us to drop out of our busy minds and beliefs into the openness and immediacy of awareness and presence, not with the idea of attaining some result or crossing a finish line, but in a spirit of never-ending discovery, and always with complete acceptance of what is, just as it is. I love the spaciousness and the simplicity I feel in his words, and his gentle and loving approach to our human struggles. If I could recommend only one book on the subject of being awake here and now, this might well be it."

—**Joan Tollifson**, teacher and author of *Nothing to Grasp*, *Awake in the Heartland*, *Painting the Sidewalk with Water*, and *Bare-Bones Meditation*

"In this wise collection of short teachings, Jon Bernie delivers the only news that's fit to print—that happiness is not something you acquire or create, but what you are fundamentally, your birthright, your natural state. Just let go of your attachment to having life be a certain way and open to the ineffable perfection of what is!"

—**Stephan Bodian**, author of *Wake Up Now* and *Beyond Mindfulness*

"There is a plethora of spiritual teachers these days. Very few actually have the gift of transmission and deep freedom. Jon has both. In person, Jon is a force of presence. I was happy to experience that coming through in this book. His words could be spoken by anyone, but they have a power in them because of where they are spoken from."

—**Megan Cowan**, cofounder of Mindful Schools

"The mark of Jon Bernie's teaching is intimacy—with his students as human beings in all their complexity, and with the Truth itself. Behind the hundreds of books and YouTube lectures on non-duality, what most of us long for is to make contact with a teacher that can directly point out the Truth as well as the very specific ways our conditioned patterns are keeping us from embodying it. Jon is such a teacher, and in *The Unbelievable Happiness of What Is*, the flavor of his work comes through crystal clear."

—**Chris McKenna**, guiding teacher of Mindful Schools

"A must-read for those on the spiritual path! I've been a devoted student of Jon Bernie's for thirty years now, and continue to attend his workshops to gain insight into the depths of the spiritual teachings he represents. I've also witnessed Jon's intense focus on studying various traditions with the greatest spiritual leaders of our time, and have seen how he has come to his own essential understandings that are so well represented in this book."

—**Daniel Kalish, DC**, founder of the Kalish Institute
    of Functional Medicine

"I highly recommend this book to others. It is a stimulating read that simplifies the life process. Bernie argues successfully that one key to Unbelievable Happiness is awakening to the moment by continually dismantling one's beliefs, routines, and any fundamental resistance to what actually is. This seemingly simple key is one of many treasures I found in Jon's book."

—**Fritz Frederick Smith, MD**, author of *Inner Bridges* and
    The Alchemy of Touch, and founder of the body-mind
    therapy, Zero Balancing

"Jon Bernie's *The Unbelievable Happiness of What Is* reminds me of Ram Dass and *Be Here Now*, the epochal, consciousness-shifting book of 1971. Like that earlier opus, Jon's work is both a restatement of ancient spiritual wisdom and a delightfully frank and open guide to modern meditative truth. Part of Jon's focus is on the core inner-growth issues of identity, identification, interpretation, integration, and belief. In Hinduism, they note that 'the first teaching is also the last teaching.' These teachings may be simple, complex, or contradictory, but they must work. And in order for them to work, they must be understandable. Jon has the gift, as teacher and as writer, of getting to the root of things in a lucid, direct way. Yet he is also able to discuss the fluid trickery of monkey mind in such a way that the monkey becomes lovable and understandable. And when we thoroughly understand something, fear and inner conflict leave, and the deeper spiritual journey can begin."

—**Hugh Milne**, author of *The Heart of Listening*

"Another book on how to find happiness? How do you choose among thousands of similar ones jostling for attention? My personal trick: a few paragraphs suffice to get a feel for the author. Can I trust that person as teacher and guide? I suggest you test this method on *The Unbelievable Happiness of What Is*. I've known Jon Bernie for a long time; I love and deeply respect him. But even if I didn't know who the author was, a page or two would suffice to make me trust someone who manages so skillfully to disappear in the process of helping me find happiness in my own way."

—**Brother David Steindl-Rast**, Benedictine monk,
author, and lecturer

"In our culture that teaches us to look outside of ourselves to consumption and materialism, in the form of buying, eating, and drugging, Jon provides us with practical guidance on ways of looking inside for the real answers that reside within us all. In our culture inundated with interruptions, Jon teaches us how to listen. In our culture that teaches us to follow others, Jon teaches us how to lead ourselves. In our culture, which is divided, Jon teaches connection through love. In the twentieth century, Ram Dass brought us *Be Here Now*. For the twenty-first century, Jon Bernie has brought us *The Unbelievable Happiness of What Is*. Read it and transform your life."

—**Richard Louis Miller, MA, PhD**, owner of
Wilbur Hot Springs

"Jon's latest book is a great reminder for the weathered seeker, as well as an incredible directive for beginners. His message and wisdom, offered in such a kind and loving way, opens the heart."

—**Cherie McCoy**, spiritual counselor and author of
Becoming Alive and Real

THE

Beyond Belief to Love,

UNBELIEVABLE

Fulfillment & Spiritual Awakening

HAPPINESS OF

JON BERNIE

WHAT IS

NON-DUALITY PRESS
An Imprint of New Harbinger Publications

Publisher's Note

This publication is designed to provide accurate and authoritative information in regard to the subject matter covered. It is sold with the understanding that the publisher is not engaged in rendering psychological, financial, legal, or other professional services. If expert assistance or counseling is needed, the services of a competent professional should be sought.

Lines from "The Question" from THE ESSENTIAL RUMI by Jalal al-Din Rumi, translated by Coleman Barks. Copyright © 1997 by Coleman Barks. Used by permission.

Distributed in Canada by Raincoast Books

Copyright © 2017 by Jon Bernie
        Non-Duality Press
        An imprint of New Harbinger Publications, Inc.
        5674 Shattuck Avenue
        Oakland, CA 94609
        www.newharbinger.com

Cover design by Amy Shoup

Acquired by Catharine Meyers

Edited by Gretel Hakanson

All Rights Reserved

FSC
www.fsc.org
MIX
Paper from responsible sources
FSC® C011935

Library of Congress Cataloging-in-Publication Data on file

19   18   17

10   9   8   7   6   5   4   3   2   1   First Printing

Contents

Foreword

We are now in the midst of a spiritual revolution in which spirit is breaking free of the various religious contexts that it has occupied for thousands of years. This has led to a flourishing of both original new teachings, as well as updated forms of traditional spirituality. In this new and evolving spiritual terrain, we are in need of wise and loving guidance more than ever, lest we lose our way amidst the tremendous influx of both new and old spiritual teachings and teachers. Ideally we need the groundedness and experience housed within the old traditions as well as the open-mindedness and dynamic expression of ever-evolving new forms of spiritual teachings and practice arising from the inspired work of modern spiritual teachers like Jon Bernie.

This delicate and important work of participating in the creation of new and inclusive forms of spiritual practice is no small task. We must all acknowledge the tendency toward magical thinking when it comes to spiritual matters and endeavor to be as clear-minded as possible in our consideration of the vast array of spiritual teachings that occupy the modern marketplace. We need not only spiritual guides of great and insightful wisdom, but also guides with an open and vulnerable heart. For the evolving spirituality of today needs to be grounded within the ancient wisdom of our spiritual traditions, while also being sensitive to the needs of human beings in the modern context of our lives.

Over the many years that I have known Jon, I have found him to embody both the depth and groundedness of traditional spiritual practice, with the openness and curiosity of a mind and heart that are creatively new, modern, and fearless. Jon is like a breath of fresh air, a light of clarity and humor shining amidst the clouds of confusion. In his own way, Jon is a groundbreaking presence of inclusion and honesty in today's crowded spiritual marketplace. He has achieved that rare human condition of being truly at peace with himself.

The book that you now hold in your hands, *The Unbelievable Happiness of What Is*, contains some of the most direct, inclusive, and useful spiritual teachings that I know of. There is no flowery spiritual lingo here, just straightforward, wise, and loving guidance for those who want to wake up from the confines of confusion and fear to whom and what they really are. And along the way, no part of the human experience is excluded or denied. Instead, every aspect of our humanity is integrated into a unifying vision of unity and love that liberates our entire being from the inside out. Such wisdom can come about only as the result of living out the journey of awakening for oneself in such a way that the totality of our human experience is grounded within the embrace of our timeless being. In short, you have to take the journey to know it. And Jon has indeed taken the journey, and it shows on every page of this book.

So I invite you not just to read through this book collecting information, but to deeply contemplate each one of its short and profound chapters. For each chapter is a fully contained teaching that needs to be digested within the silence of your being in order for it to come fully alive within you. The thing that caught my attention most about *The Unbelievable Happiness of What Is* is that the sheer and utter simplicity of our true nature is not deeply hidden in some secret place within us; it is ever present and closer than our own eyes.

> —Adyashanti
> Founder of Open Gate Sangha and author of
> *Emptiness Dancing* and *The End of Your World*

Introduction

Unbelievable Happiness

What do you really want?

I think most people would reply that they want to be happy. And isn't that the promise of awakening, of spiritual freedom, of self-realization? To be at peace, to be fulfilled. To be deeply, unconditionally happy, even amidst the changing and often challenging circumstances of our lives.

The good news is that this happiness is not something you have to accomplish. It's not something you have to get. Rather, it's something you already have. Truly, it's *what you already are.*

So why, you might ask, don't I feel this happiness? How do I access it?

The first step is simply to arrive, fully, in this moment—and to allow *what is* to be as it is, right here, right now.

In arriving fully, right now, you may find you feel alive in a way you've felt only rarely in the past, and you may get a glimpse of the possibility of awakening more deeply and permanently to your essential *being.* Once you've tasted that truth, even for just a moment, you understand inherently that in that potential transformation is a profound fullness and fulfillment that, perhaps without even realizing it, you've been seeking all your life.

As this process continues, you arrive more and more easily, and gradually what emerges is a balancing, a healing, and a transformation of the human condition. The heaviness lifts. Your heart opens. You find, shockingly, that the happiness you've been seeking has been yours all along. This is the amazing and beautiful journey that we find ourselves on together—beyond belief, beyond suffering, and beyond delusion into the unbelievable happiness of *what is*.

A MOMENT OF AWARENESS

Take a moment, right now, to check in with yourself. First, notice your surroundings—the shapes and colors of the objects around you. Notice the brightness or dimness of the light, and the shadows it casts. Notice also the sounds in your environment. Even in very quiet places, there are still sounds. Observe how those sounds come and go, shift and change, as you quietly give them your attention.

Now bring your awareness in closer, and let your attention settle into your body. Are you warm or cold? Comfortable or uncomfortable? If you're sitting in a chair, feel the chair beneath you. Feel your feet on the ground. Feel the weight of this book in your hands. Feel the temperature of the air where it touches your skin. Take a slow, deep breath, then just as slowly let it out again. Take another breath, and as you breathe out a second time, allow any tension in your body to flow out with it.

Now, if you can, let go of the breath, and see if you can let it happen on its own, without your effort or intervention. Let breathing happen by itself—*let the breath breathe you*. And as each breath moves in and out, allow your mind to relax a bit; allow your focus to loosen and settle. Allow yourself to become very, very still.

Now notice that all of this—your surroundings, the feelings in your body, the movement of your breath—all that you experience, appears within the field of your awareness. Before anything else, you are *aware*. So as the breath continues moving in and out, bring your attention now to this awareness itself—the space within which all of your experience arises. Allow yourself to relax into this awareness—to rest *as* this awareness.

In this open space of awareness, you'll find an aliveness, a brightening of experience, a vibrancy of being that may feel like a rediscovery of something you'd forgotten. This is the essence of the spiritual path—the opportunity to reconnect to this aliveness, and to allow everything that's in your way to evaporate from your system. Now your mind quiets down, your body relaxes, your heart opens, and your spirit shines, and life is an amazing, wonderful miracle—right now!

WHAT'S IN THE WAY?

So what *does* get in our way? What prevents us from seeing *what is* as it is, right now? What prevents us from being happy in this moment?

Among the biggest impediments on the spiritual path are our *unexamined beliefs* about life, about truth, and about ourselves. To be truly available for transformation, we must release ourselves from those limiting beliefs. We don't necessarily have to get rid of our beliefs; beliefs have their functions. Rather, we learn to *let go* of our beliefs, which is also to let go of our *identity*.

When I say *identity*, I mean it quite literally. Without even realizing it, you draw much of your felt sense of personal identity—that is, *who you think you are*—primarily from strongly held and often unconscious beliefs. These manifest, in part, as subtle patterns of tension and holding in your body and mind. When those beliefs are challenged, whether directly by other people or simply by the reality of changing circumstances, it can feel deeply threatening, even terrifying. In a very real sense, your beliefs define who and what you think you are, so a threat to your beliefs can feel like a threat to your very existence.

Imagine a situation in which someone calls one of your own beliefs into question. Maybe a friend suggests you're wrong about something important or a family member challenges your position on a political or social issue you care deeply about. Visualize that interaction as clearly and realistically as you can.

How do you *feel* in this moment? What sensations appear in your body? What kinds of thoughts appear in your mind—not the specific verbal content so much as the *feeling* of those thoughts? As your beliefs are called into question, do you feel anxious or frightened, or maybe defensive or angry? If so, these are your body's natural reactions to feeling threatened. But in reality, what is *actually* threatened in this kind of situation? Not your body, your human organism; not your being, your fundamental awareness—but only your beliefs.

Belief in and of itself is not a problem. Belief is fundamentally a survival mechanism, a way for the mind to organize information and make useful sense of things. It provides a kind of mental certainty that is necessary and functional at a certain level of development. But as you become more and more awake to reality itself—that is, to what's *actually real*, and actually present in your immediate, lived experience—you have less and less need for certainty. When you are truly, unconditionally *here* in this moment, your beliefs—about reality, about life, about yourself—drop away. You are simply present with what *actually is*, and you are able to respond freely, authentically, and appropriately to circumstances as they are. You have moved *beyond* belief—that is, beyond your *identity* with its self-protective mental structures you no longer need.

Now, this isn't something you can *do*, exactly—you can't just make a decision to get rid of your beliefs and take some action to force them out of existence. Rather, you can bring awareness to your beliefs and learn to observe them and let them be. Paradoxically, by bringing your beliefs into awareness and allowing them to be exactly as they are, you'll find that they begin to unwind on their own. Those patterns of tension and holding in the body and mind, both physical and energetic, will gradually dissolve and integrate back into pure awareness. There's a sort of alchemy that happens, a transmutation that can be facilitated only by this kind of application of awareness.

Of course, this isn't always as easy as it sounds! Your beliefs can be deeply anchored in your conscious and unconscious psychology, and in your physical body as well. Having your beliefs called into question can feel very threatening. So you bring awareness to that which feels threatened. I'll have a lot more to say about this later, but the essence is this: Don't try to stop yourself from feeling threatened or try to fix it somehow. Don't even try to understand why it's happening. Rather, from the space of awareness, simply observe that feeling and allow it to unwind on its own in the space that awareness creates.

LEAVING IDEAS BEHIND

You've quite possibly read all kinds of spiritual books, or heard all kinds of spiritual teachers, and as a result you may already have specific beliefs about what awakening or enlightenment is, about how it's going to unfold, about what experiences you should be having, and so on. I'm here to tell you that those beliefs are also in the way, and are, in fact, preventing you from finding your way.

Again, this isn't about not having beliefs at all, but rather about recognizing where beliefs fit into the cosmology of an open, liberated perspective. Beliefs can range from healthy to unhealthy, functional to dysfunctional, constructive to destructive. From the perspective of awareness, beliefs are respected and understood for what they are—a natural function of the human mind, useful or not useful depending on circumstance—but are not taken to be objective reflections of reality.

As I often say, beliefs are fine—as long as you don't believe them! Most people do believe their beliefs, however, and invest them with meaning, strengthening limited personal identities based on those beliefs. That produces suffering and a kind of enslavement to mental constructs that are fundamentally not true.

True happiness, true freedom, is bigger than any belief, beyond what any ideas could describe. From the perspective of pure awareness, you are no longer just this contracted, belief-based personal identity. That's not to say you won't still have an identity, a personality. Your human self will still function—in fact, it will probably function better than ever before—but it won't be identified with, won't be believed in, in the same way.

Transformation requires openness and vulnerability. For anything to open and grow, it has to be flexible. For a flower to bloom, the bud has to open. To become liberated, we must be willing to let go of who we think we are. It's that simple. "Who we think we are" is what we believe—all the stories of our history, our upbringing, our heritage; our race, religion, status, pedigree; and even our relationships, or at least our ideas about them.

A common Zen teaching describes the sage as a person of no rank. This is a description of someone who *isn't identified*. Again, that doesn't mean the sage has no personality. Awakened people can have powerful personalities that from the outside may even appear stronger than they were before awakening. No longer restricted by their beliefs or ideas about how they should be, or by worries about how others think they should be, they are free simply to show up fully and authentically as they actually are.

Let's face it—people have all kinds of beliefs about how someone who is spiritual or enlightened should appear or behave. By now you know what I'm going to say, right? Those beliefs are in the way! Most people don't get to know spiritual teachers personally as human beings, but experience them only up on the stage, or on their figurative pedestals. As a result, teachers can seem to exist in a very rarified realm, within a very narrow band of experience and behavior. But the truth is that the awakened life is rich and varied, and contains the full spectrum of human existence. If it didn't, we couldn't very well call it freedom!

Freedom is not a destination. Awakening has no endpoint. How could there be an endpoint in an infinitely expanding universe? Where is this end, and where was the beginning? If we're honest with ourselves, we'll see clearly that we really don't have that kind of certainty about *anything*. We actually have no idea what's going on!

BEYOND BELIEF

Freedom, true freedom, is literally beyond belief. As you deepen in this process, you leave belief way behind. You leave dogma way behind. You leave teachings and teachers behind. You arrive fully in this moment, unfettered by anything you've known or assumed before.

As gradually you begin to relinquish your attachment to the limited self you've taken yourself to be, you become integrated and balanced, and a deep healing becomes available to you. You begin to really live from your heart. You listen from your heart. You *feel* from your heart. We feel each other, profoundly. We are one in the Heart of Vastness—this vast field of awareness and presence that is common to all of us.

What's most important on this path is simply to learn to be available to your own experience—and to get out of your own way! Of course you first need to be able to see that you are *in* the way, so being honest with yourself is essential. As you meet challenges along the way, I invite you also to have some compassion for yourself, and for your own struggle. Human beings are human beings! You're not going to be perfect. You're not going to be flawless. But this path isn't about becoming something you're not. It's not about transcending the human condition, but about embracing it—about becoming *fully* human.

In an awakened, fully integrated life, everything is welcomed. Nothing is excluded. Everything can be recycled and transformed. So let your light shine! Let your heart open. Drop your walls, drop your barriers, and most of all, drop your beliefs. Then the true richness and depth of life will be obvious and available, regardless of what's happening around you.

Now you're free of getting somewhere. You're free of getting something. You're free of being somebody. You're free of the past, free of the future. Now you get to have your life, finally, as it *actually is* in each moment. You arrive in this moment to find out that you've always been here—that this natural being, this profound stillness and ease, is what you *already are*. You didn't have to accomplish it; you only needed to let it arrive, and let it liberate you. That's what surrender really means—dropping your guard, relaxing your defenses, and *allowing* yourself to be liberated.

To awaken is really to become fully alive—to *live fully each moment* in being. In that *beingness* you find, finally, the meaning and purpose of your life.

How to Read This Book

You may have read other spiritual books or heard other spiritual teachings, and as a result you may already have your own ideas about what words like "awakening," "freedom," and "liberation" mean. I invite you now to drop those ideas, all those definitions, and allow yourself to start fresh. See if you can let yourself encounter all of the words and concepts in this book as if hearing them for the first time.

You may find that my use of terminology is not always precise, and that I sometimes use different words for the same ideas at different times, or describe things from different angles or different perspectives. Language is inherently limited, but what we're talking about here is unlimited, and in truth unknowable. As a result, linguistic descriptions will always be approximate, and any definitions tentative and open to exploration.

So the ideas and suggestions I'm offering in this book are not intended as descriptions of how things are or of a "way" or a particular set of methods you should follow. Rather, they are intended as pointers, tips, and guidelines to help you discover your *own* way, in your own experience.

As you sit down to read, take a moment to get centered in your body. Spend a little time stopping, breathing. Be quiet, even if for just a few moments, so that your mind can unwind and your emotions can settle down a bit. Let yourself relax. Let yourself center.

As you read, you might have reactions to what you're reading. You may find yourself surprised, delighted, challenged, or comforted—or irritated! You may find yourself making judgments or drawing conclusions. And that's fine! As those things happen, notice what happens in your body. Notice any feelings that arise. Notice also the mental content of your reactions. Do you find yourself agreeing or disagreeing? Does something inspire you? Does something else trigger you?

How you are reacting is actually not that important. What is key is becoming *aware* of your reactions as they happen and noticing the changes in your body that go along with them.

You also don't need to "understand" what I'm saying on an intellectual level. So I invite you to come to this book with the very attitude "I don't need to understand." If something I say doesn't make sense to you, don't worry about it! Rather, notice how you *feel* about it not making sense, notice how that experience impacts you, and then read on!

Overall, be gentle with yourself. You don't have to get it. You don't have to understand it. You can't do it wrong! So take it easy. Relax, and enjoy the journey.

Let's begin.

1.

Taking the First Step

If you can *listen* into the silence beneath these words, that's the first step. If you can *see* what's actually in front of you, right now, *that's* the first step. If you can relax into your body and really *feel* the sensations that are present for you here in this moment, *that's* the first step. And you only need to take one step!

In fact, it's not even a step—you don't have to go anywhere. Simply *being here* with what is, as it is, is fundamentally radical. It precedes going. It precedes doing. It precedes being someone. It leads to the dropping away of the veil of our *belief* that we are only this limited, specific person, with a history, with a past and a future— and to the understanding that what we *truly* are is free of all of that.

With that one step, we enter into this brilliant space of unraveling, of unwinding, where we find out what it truly means to be free and at peace, whatever our external circumstances. In this open space of pure awareness, what arises just arises, whether that's joy, pain, bliss, or sadness. We learn to allow these movements without being caught by them, without feeling the need to grasp, resist, or even understand them. We learn to *listen into the silence* beneath these movements, the silence that's present even when words are being spoken.

Although people often approach me as a teacher, the truth is that I'm not actually teaching anything. There's nothing to teach. There's nothing to learn. There's only waking up to what's *actually present* right now.

It's important to understand that I don't mean "waking up" to some collection of ideas about being awake or free. Memorizing or "understanding" concepts about enlightenment might help you create a new set of beliefs, but the only thing that will believe them—the only thing that *has* belief—is the limited personal self you've mistakenly taken yourself to be. That which you *truly* are does not believe anything. Awareness itself does not have an identity called "spiritually awake" or "liberated."

But even though "teaching" is in some sense an illusion, there is nevertheless value in coming together with others on the path, whether in person or by reading books like this one. In this way we connect and find common ground with people who are conscious in a way that allows us to find our own consciousness. By connecting to others, we connect to ourselves, and to the Big Self—this vast field of awareness that we all share—and gradually we come to understand in the marrow of our bones that we are not separate from each other, and never have been.

You and I may not know each other personally, but even so, I think you'll find there's a sense of familiarity between us, an awareness that knows itself in the other, even at a distance. Even when our "interaction" is only through your reading of this book, there's nevertheless a kind of union that happens—with each other, with ourselves, and with all things.

◇◇◇◇

This isn't about reading or hearing some teaching you've never heard before. You've probably heard them *all* before! It's fine to hear teachings, of course; that can be helpful and even essential at certain points in your development. But this is a hands-on school. This is about jumping into the river, about climbing the mountain, about *direct experience*.

This is also not about learning some particular set of methods or techniques. Fundamentally, I emphasize simply resting in awareness, presence, consciousness itself. Traditionally this is called the *direct path*—getting right to the essence behind all forms, behind all ideas and concepts.

Even so, there are things you can do to get you oriented in the right direction, ways you can set yourself up to allow transformation to happen. Throughout this book I'll be offering pointers and suggestions, practices and inquiries you can try on for yourself. I invite you to explore these in whatever way and at whatever pace is comfortable for you. Some of my suggestions may resonate for you, some may not, and that's completely fine! There's no one-size-fits-all approach to awakening.

Ultimately I'm here to help you find your *own* way. My role is to support you in finding out how to live your own life authentically and fully, as you deepen into the mystery and the uncertainty and the unbelievable happiness of *not knowing*.

◇◇◇◇

Awareness itself is the key to really understanding the truth. In a very real sense, it *is* the truth itself. Awareness is inexplicable, beyond our cognitive functioning—beyond belief!—and yet it permeates everything. Really *being* here, dropping in, and allowing that awareness to grow us, or cultivate us, or cook us, facilitates the unfolding of the spirit and the heart.

A famous and often-quoted Zen teaching states that there's *nowhere to go*, and *nothing to do*. From a conventional perspective, those may seem like negative statements, but they're really quite the opposite. There's nowhere to go because there's *only here*. There's nothing to do because it's already done! What could be more positive than that? So just *be* here. Relax and let yourself ground. Open to what's *actually happening* right here, right now.

It can sometimes help to ask yourself questions: "How am I available for *whatever* is happening, however it is, right now? Without judgments, conclusions, or comparisons, how can I simply perceive this moment as it is?" That which *allows* it to be as it is, right now, is awareness, your true nature. Awareness is non-grasping, non-volitional. It isn't trying to be someone. It isn't trying get something. It just *is*.

So drop out of your mind and into your heart, into your body, into your breath. Drop into *being here*. Notice the movements of your mind in response—does it try to reassert control; does it try to dominate? If it does, see if you can give yourself a little tender loving care, a little compassion, forgiveness, and gratitude, just for being able to be here, even if being here is uncomfortable or not what you wish it was.

Let's face it: "Here" isn't always how you want it to be! So the path to freedom is to find the "here" that's *free* of how you want it to be, that's free of being anything in particular—that's free of being anything at all! Any moment in which you are fully here without wanting "here" to be somewhere else, you are free. So *any* moment can be a moment of freedom.

These moments of freedom may seem fleeting at first, but as you learn to recognize them, they'll last longer and come more often. Eventually, freedom will be your default setting, your natural resting state. So catch these moments. Notice them. Appreciate them. And if they're fleeting, no blame! No problem. You'll arrive back here again soon enough.

One of the primary characteristics of our true nature is infinite patience. Awareness doesn't have a watch. It doesn't have a calendar. Each moment is a brand-new opportunity to arrive. So let your heart be soft. Let it be vulnerable. Allow yourself to settle, to relax and center. Soon you'll find you are moving quite naturally from being heavy, burdened, and dense to being light, effortless, and open.

2.

Path of the Heart

I'd like to invite you to make yourself at home. Take a moment right now and breathe in, deeply. Really *feel* the sensations of your belly expanding, your chest rising, your lungs filling with air. Now relax, and let your chest fall, your lungs empty, and your body loosen and settle. Take another deep breath, all the way in, and then relax and let it out again. Now let your breath continue on its own, and bring your attention to your chest. Settle there. Rest in the center of your heart. Find your home ground, right here, right now.

It's so much easier to follow the path of the heart than to try to follow the path of the knowing mind. Through the doorway of the personal heart, you can enter what I call the Heart of Vastness, or the Big Heart of infinite connection. Later, of course, you can bring the mind back, and it can be very useful. So long as it's not in the driver's seat, the mind can be a brilliant vehicle of creative intelligence, rather than serving as the voice of your dominating will. Then expression becomes poetry. Or, better yet, comedy!

But right now, tune in to your heart. Is it at peace, or is it in some healing process? Are expansion and opening happening, or do you feel contraction or holding on? What else is happening in your body right now? What sensations, what feelings? Finding your home ground has to begin with the body—with the movement of the breath, the feelings of the heart, all the natural rhythms of this mysterious, miraculous life form you find yourself inhabiting.

◇◇◇◇

The path of the heart is to learn to listen, rather than talk; to allow, rather than dominate; and to really take in the many, many communications from all directions that are guiding your attention, helping show you the way to return home.

That guidance, that inherent wisdom, is always communicating, always and forever attempting to return you to wakefulness. So even in those inevitable times when you're quite out of balance, it's helpful to allow yourself to *feel* the imbalance, the disconnectedness, the off-centeredness. Gradually you'll learn to allow your experience to be *exactly as it is*, rather than trying to avoid it, or fix it, or even understand it.

Allowing yourself to be out of balance is often how balance can return. The great Zen master Dogen Zenji described human life as "one continuous mistake." If it wasn't, he asked, how would we find our way? Most people think mistakes are to be avoided, but on the spiritual path, mistakes are welcomed. So-called mistakes are opportunities, guideposts, lights illuminating our way.

So the path is to turn *toward* what's difficult and allow it to guide you. Gradually you learn to understand and accept that you're always in the midst of ongoing transformation. Even when you feel stuck, caught in the drama and struggle of the identified, suffering, separate self—even then transformation is actually in process.

Spirituality does not mean leaving your humanity behind. Rather, the height of spirituality is the *complete embrace* of every aspect of your humanity. Many people believe being "spiritual" means transcending our humanity, somehow escaping our flawed and messy human experience. But true spirituality is the opposite of that. Nothing is denied. Nothing is excluded. How could it be? Ultimately, what else is there but this simple, human experience that is the only reality we know?

Each year I lead several meditation retreats, which are held mostly in silence. A few days into any given retreat, as the silence deepens, there's sometimes a moment when I hit the bell to signal the end of a meditation period, and yet no one moves. The stillness has become so deep, the sense of ease so profound, that there really is, as that famous Zen teaching says, "Nowhere to go" and "Nothing to do," and that realization produces not boredom or lethargy, but rather a profound sense of being deeply, incredibly, unbelievably at home. That's arriving—really arriving.

Now, if you've never been on a silent retreat, this may sound exotic and unusual, but whether you realize it or not, you already know that silence, that stillness. It is your very nature, the essence of your being. You only need to learn to recognize it and to trust the guidance that arises from that stillness and points to the truth that is within you—that *is* you.

As we integrate this truth, this vast peace that we are, we begin to welcome anything that might be challenging us—any difficulties we may be faced with in our work, our relationships, our health, our financial situations. We finally have the space to really take care of whatever needs to be taken care of, right here, right now. From this space of acceptance, we find out how to truly live, how to be in this world, and how to be of service to others.

When we can really tune in, allow, and listen, completely surrendering into that vast space of the heart, we find it's a total joy to be here. It's such an incredible pleasure simply to be alive, and yet this unbelievable richness is nothing that needs to be held onto at all. It's just one discovery after another, one surprise after another, one revelation after another.

◇◇◇◇

It can be very beneficial to spend time with others who are on this path and who are also exploring and resonating on this frequency of being. So I invite you to reach out and connect, in whatever way seems right for you. That shared resonance can be deeply supportive as each of us finds our respective way. We see the light in each other. We feel the love of our one heart, and it's a blessing! It brings out gratitude and appreciation, and a deep understanding that the true purpose of life is to *be here*, completely, with no holding back—to be fully at home, right now.

The happiest we as human beings can be is when we're in love at the highest level, and this awareness we're cultivating together engenders that love and brings it forth. It's very easy to lose our sense of meaning as human beings, to feel alienated, disconnected, or disenfranchised, particularly in the face of all that seems wrong in the world. But as this understanding blooms in you, you'll know— without believing!—the meaning and purpose of your life. In that knowing, you will find a fulfillment that is relaxed and effortless, and that will gradually become your refuge, your resting place—your true home ground of being.

3.

Path of Least Resistance

The path of the heart is also the *path of least resistance*. Awakening is a natural force, and we want to allow ourselves to *align* with that force rather than resisting it.

The path of least resistance is to be fully conscious, yet free of any effort. Otherwise you're coming from the perspective of the separate self, where there's *someone* who's *trying* to be conscious. Although that might feel like well-directed effort, it's actually resistance. It's using the *idea* of "being conscious" to resist what's *actually* happening—which may be different from your idea! When you drop that resistance, even for just a moment, the separate self is no longer in the driver's seat, and real consciousness becomes available.

The path of least resistance is not necessarily easy. It could actually be quite difficult because we're so conditioned to resist and defend against what we don't want to feel. Awakening challenges this resistance. It's almost like a psychic lubricant; as awareness begins to permeate deeper parts of ourselves that have gone unexamined for a very long time, we suddenly find things moving that we didn't expect, things we didn't necessarily expect or want to move. *Wait a minute*, we may think, *this isn't what I signed up for!*

But as you gradually deepen into awareness—as you become *embodied* in awareness—presence becomes your default setting, and resistance is no longer what's happening for you. Eventually there's no longer even the impulse to resist, to go back; presence is just where you are.

Of course there may still be what I like to call "ego flare-ups," but that's inevitable and entirely to be expected. It's just the chickens coming home to roost. Eventually all your scattered parts—the parts of you that have been repressed, cut off, marginalized, or just forgotten—return home to be integrated. They come back to be forgiven, to be loved, to be embraced—and finally to be appreciated because they are the fuel for the fire of transformation.

So cease to turn away from what's difficult and learn to turn toward it instead, with the fullness of heart and the tenderness of body that vulnerability requires. The vulnerability of transformation requires softness and tenderness. It requires getting out of the way and letting go of control. It requires questioning beliefs—and having the willingness to not know what's going on! And to not be anxious about not knowing what's going on or what's going to happen next.

Real transformation requires the willingness to be fully and completely human—to have feelings, to let the heart move its energies as it needs to, and to listen to the body when it's communicating its needs or its limitations. We begin to respect this temple that we've been given, miraculously and unknowingly. How did we get here? We don't know; we *can't* know. It's a truly mind-blowing mystery. So we begin to have real reverence for this life because at any moment, this bubble can pop. This existence will be gone.

The old schools of spiritual teaching were often about transcending our human nature, but by this point you're probably beginning to understand that this school is about *embracing* it. We're not throwing out the garbage; we're recycling it, reclaiming all the parts of ourselves we'd previously repressed, rejected, or pushed aside. We're offering those parts our forgiveness and compassion—and ultimately, our gratitude and appreciation.

Our humanity, with all its difficulties and limitations, is part of the universal function, an essential and necessary element of the ecosystem of life and freedom. *Whatever* is present, believe it or not, will lead you home to freedom. As you gradually come to understand how that process works, you can relax and find comfort in simply trusting that guidance will show you the way home.

Freedom is *right here*. It isn't something that will happen in the future. It isn't something you missed in the past. It's right here, right now, and always has been. This understanding, this deep knowing, is already and profoundly *what you are*. In fact, it's what everything is. It is the creative intelligence, the life force that animates this mysterious, infinite universe. When you align with that knowing, when it becomes deeply integrated, you can really enjoy each moment and be fully available for whatever is needed. To recognize the truth is to *become* the truth, and *that* is the path of least resistance, from the beginning, to the middle, to the end.

4.

Simply Bringing Attention

As human beings, we have a lot of practical understanding—a lot of experience, a lot of intelligence, a lot of knowledge. Our minds can do amazing things. But that's not the kind of understanding I'm pointing to in this book. What I'm talking about is radiant awareness: the pure, creative, intelligent force that animates this universe. We can call it awareness, God, divine consciousness... We have so many names for it, but ultimately we don't know what it is. And yet, *we are that.*

There's a place for knowing about and understanding things on an intellectual level, certainly. This is where it's important to distinguish clearly as to whether we're speaking relatively or absolutely. On the relative level, practical knowledge is of course very useful. What to eat, how to do your job, how to take care of yourself on a human level—these are obviously areas where specific practical knowledge is essential.

The teaching I'm conveying in this book, however, is not fundamentally about practical functioning. This is about becoming liberated, about becoming truly and unconditionally happy, and in that realm—the realm of opening, expanding, and letting go—knowing from the mental perspective can often be a kind of restriction.

"Knowing" about spirituality—the accumulation of spiritual concepts, ideas about what spiritual progress or spiritual realization looks like—can be used by the separate, identified self as a defense against real transformation. Of course spiritual concepts and knowledge can be useful at certain points on the path. They can inspire us and help keep us focused and motivated. But ultimately, spiritual concepts must be discarded along with all other limiting ideas. Otherwise they can form a kind of "spiritual" identity, which can be very difficult to extricate oneself from.

So there's certainly a place for knowing and understanding on a practical level and on an intellectual level. But when it comes to real transformation, the truth lies in *not knowing*—in leaving all your ideas and concepts about spirituality behind and allowing yourself to rest in the direct experience of reality itself, beyond all ideas and concepts.

◇◇◇◇

I want to introduce what might be the most basic practice of all, which is *simply bringing attention to what's happening*.

Take a moment when you're alone, sitting in your room. You're not listening to music, not watching television. You're not interacting with another person. You're just sitting quietly.

Now *look*, and let there be *just looking*. Let yourself simply *see* what's in front of you—without thinking about it, without labeling it, without *knowing* anything about it. If there's furniture in front of you, for instance, don't think *furniture* or *chair*, or that it's covered in leather or cloth, or that it's this or that color. Rather, let yourself simply see what's there, without projections, preconceptions, or interpretations, as if you had never seen anything like it before.

Now turn your attention to sound. Listen, and let there be *just listening*. Whether what you're hearing is people nearby, traffic, birds, or the sounds of nature—from your perspective there's just sound. Don't think, *There goes a car driving by*, or *There are some birds*, or *There are some people talking*. Let yourself simply experience those sounds—as if you had never heard sounds like those before—and without attaching any meaning to those sounds.

Now notice your bodily sensations—the feeling of the cushions you're sitting on, or the clothes you're wearing, or the temperature of the room, but again, without labeling, interpreting, evaluating, or judging. Allow yourself to just have the pure, simple experience of being where you are, right now.

Notice that when you are fully present with your experience in this way, your senses envelop your attention completely, and your mind, even if for just a moment, is quiet. The "knower"—the one that thinks, that understands, that problem solves—drops away. The filter of the separate self, at least for this moment, ceases to function.

To be fully present to your senses—without resisting, without grasping, without defensiveness or offensiveness—facilitates real presence, the purest form of our *being*. You are completely absorbed in the present moment.

So try it. Let seeing envelop you. Let hearing envelop you. Let any or all of your five senses envelop you fully. Let *knowing* drop away, and simply be here with what is, as it is.

You don't need to be alone in your home to do this. At any moment, in almost any situation, you can take a break from thinking and come back into your body, tune in to your senses, and arrive back in this moment.

When eating, for instance, you might take a bite of fruit—a strawberry, say, or a piece of papaya or banana—and let yourself really experience the flavor, the texture, the smell. Rather than thinking *papaya* or *banana*, instead allow the immediate sensory experience of it to envelop your attention.

When walking, relax and just be aware of walking—of the sensations of your legs moving, your arms swinging, of the sights and sounds and feelings you're experiencing. Even during very complex activity, like running or bicycling or playing a musical instrument, you can actually find this presence and stillness in the midst of that movement.

◇◇◇◇

As your attention becomes more refined over time, you'll notice there are different ways to bring attention, different flavors of awareness. You can apply a very finely focused, laser-point concentration—not by forcing yourself to concentrate, but rather by *allowing* your attention to settle to a very fine point, in a sense relaxing into one-pointedness. Or you can really open up the lens and allow your attention to become global, all-encompassing, so that you're aware of nothing in particular, and yet of everything at once.

This is where I encourage you to experiment. Don't just do it one way. Try different approaches, and notice which you prefer. Notice what you're doing and how you are doing it, and most importantly, notice the result! Does what you're doing leave you feeling more open or more contracted? Notice also how the simple act of examining your experience in this way can itself move you more into openness.

You might even get in the habit of trying this whenever you find yourself stretched, or stressed, or overwhelmed. Train yourself to develop a certain sensitivity to those things, such that if you find yourself in a struggle, you take that as a signal to stop, check in with yourself, and tune in to your body. Drop the mental chatter, the worry, the stress, the story, and instead arrive back here in this moment.

I try to help people learn to trust their experience, deeply. This is very different from knowing or *believing* something about it. To trust your experience means to surrender to it, to cease resisting. When resistance truly ceases, you're vulnerable, you're available, and your heart is ready to open.

5.

The Positive Side of Belief

I often talk about the freedom of *not knowing*, or not believing. Before we go any further, though, I want to also say something about the positive aspects of knowing and believing. As long as you remain identified to some extent, then knowing and believing are going to be part of your experience—and that's not all bad!

Consider, for instance, the placebo effect. People who believe they've been given an analgesic will often experience a reduction in physical pain, even when what they've really been given is only a sugar pill. Belief is very powerful. How you think and what you believe affect you profoundly, so your expectations in different situations can produce very different experiences.

So while true spiritual insight is *beyond* the realm of belief, you nevertheless don't want to throw the baby out with the bathwater. As long as you do still have beliefs, there's definitely something to be said for having beliefs that are helpful rather than unhelpful.

I frequently work with people to help them identify the unhelpful or limiting ways they may be seeing or framing their experience, and to help them develop the ability to shift that framing in ways that are more useful and supportive. It can be very helpful to become conscious of the attitudes with which you approach your experience, to identify just what you do believe, and to learn to shift or reframe those attitudes and beliefs if they're not serving you.

So I want to be clear that what I'm offering in this book is not a rejection of thought or belief *per se*. When I speak of freeing yourself from belief, I don't mean you necessarily need to eliminate your beliefs altogether. Rather, to free yourself from belief is to let go of your *identity* with your beliefs. Now you've dropped the burden of *being* the knower—of *being* the one who hides in knowing, who uses knowing as a kind of shield. Knowing and believing may still be part of your experience, but they're no longer a problem, no longer a cause of suffering—and importantly, when your beliefs are challenged, it's no longer experienced as threatening. At times you might even find it delightful!

Awakening is really about that shift of identity from *being* the separate, limited self that believes to instead *being* the pure awareness within which that self arises. From that perspective there is no knower. There is no knowing. There is no believing. There's no one *to* believe. There's only this moment as it presents itself in the field of your awareness.

But you can't orchestrate that shift by forcing yourself to drop your beliefs or to let go of knowing. Rather, you learn to notice the impact of your knowing and believing. You observe how belief operates, how it affects your experience. You see where it gets in the way of opening, and also where it doesn't. As you see this more clearly, then gradually the identity with belief falls away on its own. You don't necessarily even notice at first, but at some point you suddenly realize that something is missing. You haven't gained anything, but rather something that was present before is now absent—and that absence is a great relief!

When in my own journey I came to that transition, it was a 180-degree shift in my understanding of who I was and what I was. I no longer knew anything. I no longer believed anything. For me this was remarkable because I had been *very* identified with knowing and believing! I was what you might call a competitive spiritual seeker—I read every book I could, and spent endless hours studying and collecting information about spirituality. After all, I wanted to be free! I didn't realize that in a very subtle way I was actually increasing my burden rather than decreasing it.

But after awakening, that need to know was gone, and as the burden of all that knowing lifted, what I found instead was a profound openness and an incredible lightness of being. For a time I felt weightless. It was like I was floating, not even touching the ground. It was amazing.

For a few people this transition happens suddenly, and I'm sure you've heard some of their stories. For most, though, it's a more gradual, incremental process—and that's a good thing! Sudden, explosive transformations can be messy. If you planted an acorn in your yard and it became a gigantic oak tree overnight, the effect on the rest of your yard might not be quite what you were hoping for.

However it shows up for you over time, in whatever way it emerges, when presence becomes foreground in your experience—even for just a moment—*that's* what you want to give attention to. Relax into that awareness. Surrender to it. Give yourself to it. Appreciate it. Love it! However you choose to think about it, simply allow that presence to be in consciousness.

As this process deepens for you, be gentle with yourself. Have some compassion for the limited personal self that's done its best to take care of you, to keep you safe and protected. Although the essence of this path is learning to recognize our true nature as consciousness itself, in that recognition, we also learn how to allow the healing of the human self that still knows and believes. We learn how to work with the movement and struggles of the conditional personal self. We learn to allow and accept even its dark side so it can heal and be released and integrated.

In that acceptance, the identity of the knower is released. That release comes not as the result of your *trying* to be free, trying to become enlightened, but simply through allowing the natural movement of awareness, deepening into itself. As that movement matures and deepens, you might find yourself observing, "I am this presence. I am awareness itself." Or you might just enjoy it—the love, the light, the connectedness, and the amazing fullness that is each and every moment.

THE UNBELIEVABLE HAPPINESS OF WHAT IS

Every moment of awareness is a moment of *not knowing*—a moment of freedom, a glimpse of the truth. Every moment of it nourishes you and moves you in the direction of transformation, and you'll be amazed to discover that no effort on your part is required for that to happen. No knowledge is required. No understanding is required. You only need to allow *what is* to be as it is. Awakening is already yours, already available to you right here, right now. You only need to *let it happen*.

6.

What Is Awakening?

One of my most important teachers was a man named Jean Klein. When I first met him back in the late 1980s, he immediately said to me, "You don't need any intellectual input." I said, "I know! I can't read spiritual books anymore. I read one line and immediately fall asleep." We cracked up laughing. Then I said, "I can't even read *your* books!" And we laughed again because he knew that I was already receiving the teaching that is, and can only be, transmitted tacitly in the silence.

So what does it mean to receive the teaching? What is it that's transmitted? What *is* awakening? Depending on where you are in your own process, the so-called answer may be less useful than the question itself.

This very natural and very common discovery we call awakening is really just the ongoing process of opening to a much bigger perspective of this mystery we call life, and paradoxically, as you explore more and more deeply you'll find that existence becomes *more* mysterious rather than less!

So rather than seeking an answer, embrace the question. Rest in the question. *Live* the question. Gradually your identity will shift from the form—the limited person you've always taken yourself to be, with its history and personality, its dramas and struggles—to the emptiness, the space within which that personality has arisen, within which that history and all those dramas and struggles have played out. You'll move from closedness to openness, from knowing to *not knowing*.

Awakening is active. It's being open*ing* rather than a passive state of being open. It's a movement of energy, of availability, of receptivity—and when you are truly receptive, you are also radiant, transmitting the truth of who and what you are in every moment.

Awakening is not an endpoint. It's an ongoing discovery, an ongoing movement into the perpetual unknown. In an infinite, unknowable universe how could there *be* an endpoint? The *idea* of an endpoint, a place called "awakening" that you're striving to reach, might be useful temporarily; the sense of a goal or destination could be a helpful motivating idea, especially as you're just starting out on the path. But ultimately, awakening is not an idea. It cannot be understood or comprehended through thinking. Thinking may have gotten you in the door, but now you have to find out how to let go of thinking, how to allow yourself to dissolve into this vastness of pure presence.

If you can allow yourself to *just be here*, that dissolving will happen quite naturally. For most people this happens gradually, over time, but even so you may find the effects of that dissolving showing up more quickly than you expect.

As you deepen and become embodied in presence, you'll also begin to see clearly where you're still caught or struggling. The ways you've been conditioned to protect and defend yourself will become obvious, and those too will begin to dissolve. As gradually you relinquish your many strategies of protection and separation, a deep movement of healing and integration will begin to emerge by itself.

Contrary to popular belief, awakening is the *beginning* of the path, not the end. Awakening continues to unfold and expand, and gradually the human person transforms and heals. From that awakened perspective, life—even with all of its complexities, disappointments, and unfulfilled dreams—has profound meaning. There's a richness, right here, and you might even say that you *are* that richness.

You already know what I'm talking about. Whether you're aware of it or not, at some point in your life, you've had at least a glimpse, a taste, of that possibility. It's built in—that wisdom is just part of this life. It's not something that you don't have and you need to get, or that someone else has and you don't. If some teacher is telling you it is, that's your signal to run in the opposite direction as quickly as possible!

So how do you find awakening? The answer is in the silence. It's in the stillness. It's in stopping and simply allowing this moment to reveal itself. It's in finding out how to become available for *it* to find *you*.

As you tune in to this moment, you may experience a natural expansiveness, which can feel very nice, but tuning in deeply could also activate things in you that have been hidden or held in. You may find that some emotional or physical pain that's gone unseen or unacknowledged now comes into view, and it may be difficult to allow that emergence to happen. But that's okay! If you find yourself resisting, take a step back and simply notice that resistance. That is to say, allow what's happening—even if what's happening is *not allowing*! Be the space within which *not allowing* is happening.

Many of us have been so hard on ourselves in this life, blaming ourselves for our shortcomings and limitations. Now, from the awakened perspective, we finally learn to engender and nurture compassion for the limited, imperfect, and sometimes wounded and broken human beings that we are. We begin to develop care and tenderness, forgiveness and patience, and love for ourselves. From infinite spacious awareness, everything is allowed. The heart can finally be heard, can finally be healed. We can finally be fully acknowledged. I think what we all deeply seek as human beings, probably more than anything, is to be loved—and to love.

Awakening leads to the opening, healing, and liberation of the heart. The heart is a very delicate flower, but when it blooms, it's the most beautiful and fragrant flower of all.

◇◇◇◇

Your fundamental nature is fulfillment—not the fulfillment of getting your needs met or accomplishing your goals, but the fulfillment of the *fullness of being*. That's why we're here—to discover that and to rediscover it in each and every moment. Awareness is always present and always available, but how to locate it may not always be obvious to us. So we seek out help. We look for teachers and teachings to help us find our original nature—to have it mirrored, to have it reflected back to us. To honor it, to give ourselves to it. To help us simply relax into that effortless ease of being.

And then what? We just live our lives! We hang out with our friends; we enjoy ourselves. No longer caught in the illusion of being separate, we find out in each moment how to allow the creative maturing process of this human mystery to unfold. Life becomes endlessly interesting, a realm of infinite discovery even in the simplest of activities—washing the dishes, taking out the garbage, brushing your teeth—and there is profound joy in the simplicity of each moment.

7.

The Essence of Meditation

Many people who come to hear me speak, work with me privately, or come on my retreats have already been involved with spiritual practices of various kinds. Often they've had at least some meditation training or been on a few retreats. So although in the past I did sometimes lead introductory meditation classes and retreats, more recently I haven't usually offered generalized meditation instructions unless someone specifically asks for that kind of support. I've found that the teaching I offer can work with whatever practices people are doing.

Even so, I do try to help people calibrate their own practice or approach. For some people this may mean recommending they take up a regular sitting practice for the first time, while for others it could mean suggesting they ease off their long-time practice and instead focus on cultivating small moments of awareness throughout the day. Yet others may benefit more from taking up a qigong practice or another body-oriented therapy or practice. There's really no one-size-fits-all approach.

Generally speaking, I try to empower people to experiment and find out what works best for them. The guiding principle is always the direct experience of presence—I invite people to notice how whatever practice they're doing either facilitates or restricts that experience for them. For instance, maybe you already have a practice of your own. If the net effect of your practice is that you feel more relaxed, more open, more expanded, then I would say that practice is working. If on the other hand you feel more contracted over time, then it's probably time to look at changing your approach.

For most people, meditation practice can be very helpful in developing the ability to relax the mind and open the channels of the body, allowing freer movement of energy and often more harmonious states of mind. So whether you personally have meditated for years or are just considering taking up a practice for the first time, I'll offer here a few broad guidelines, pointers that might help you find your way, tools you can experiment with in your own spiritual laboratory.

◇◇◇◇

I generally recommend a particular qigong-based sitting posture because I find that most people need to clear stuck energy more than they need to get concentrated. So instead of the traditional approach of sitting on a cushion on the floor, try sitting on a chair. Place your feet flat on the ground and your hands flat on your legs, palms facing downward.

If you can, allow your spine to be erect, but without tightening your torso or holding yourself rigidly in a particular position. See if you can find a relaxed posture where your upper body can balance on your hip sockets. You may want to sit so that your knees are slightly lower than your hips; sometimes people find that helps them balance without tension. Allow your head to be balanced on top of your spine rather than pulled back. Relax your neck and move your head back and forth very gently, very subtly—side to side, forward and back—until you find a place where the head feels relaxed and balanced atop the spine.

If you have back issues or find that sitting like this strains your body in some way, then experiment with different ways of sitting, different chairs, or different arrangements of cushions. There are all kinds of options you can play with to find the optimal sitting support.

Once you are sitting comfortably, take a deep breath, and then slowly let it out again. Rest your attention about three finger-widths below your navel, and now simply watch or sense your breath moving in and moving out. Allow the breath to rise and fall on its own, without effort, without interference. *Let the breath breathe you.* If thoughts or mental activity pull you away, then as you notice that, gently redirect your attention back to the movement of the breath, there in your belly, just below the navel.

Sit quietly—breath moving in, breath moving out—for as long or short a time as you like. If meditation is new for you, maybe try just a few minutes at first. Over time try longer intervals if you're comfortable with that. Try different lengths of time and different times of day. Again, experiment and find out what works for you.

As you sit, see what you observe. If you find yourself being reactive or judgmental toward yourself, I encourage you to offer yourself some compassion, patience, forgiveness, and gratitude. Cut yourself some slack! Give yourself a break. It's very important to be kind to yourself.

◇◇◇◇

Certain attitudes or qualities of attention can help you on this path. I've often suggested that the two attitudes most helpful to cultivate are those of the *explorer* and those of the *scientist*. The explorer wanders boldly in undiscovered territory, never knowing what they'll encounter next, while the scientist observes what's happening with precise attention and no preconceptions, all the while *questioning everything*.

With curiosity and an open heart and open mind, you can be flexible enough to actually learn. You won't be caught holding on to some idea about who you are or how you're supposed to be.

It's also important to explore and work with your attitude, your perspective on what are you doing here. One of the biggest internal barriers you can have is to think you know what's happening, or what should be happening. Maybe you're comparing what's happening with what you've experienced before, or with what you've heard about some other person's practice or so-called enlightenment experience. Be careful! Thinking you know what should be happening will prevent you from being with what's *actually* happening.

Remember: You're not doing this to get to somewhere else. The only place you're going to get to is *here*. Most people aren't really here, or they're very minimally here. So most of these kinds of practices are oriented toward *becoming fully here*. As you become more available to the present moment, your awareness will begin to expand and open, and what you'll experience then may surprise you.

A problem that arises with many practices is that people get stuck in the form—they fixate on the mechanics of "being mindful" or doing concentration. As they get better at the technique, they may learn to cultivate a sort of buzz, a slightly altered state that does have a certain quality of presence, but is also somewhat limited, and a little inflexible. They may find themselves trying to hold on to this experience—"being very mindful"—and may get a bit rigid around it. And actually, that's fine! It's okay for a while, and even a necessary phase for many people. No blame, no shame.

Ultimately, though, you need to give yourself permission to be creative, to explore, to try different things, and to not worry about getting it right or about having some particular experience. It's really important to know that you can't get this wrong! It's okay to be human. It's okay to have whatever condition, whatever struggle is arising right now.

Often when someone begins a sitting practice, they quickly find out that they've never really been present in their body—that they're always in their head, lost in some mental world. If you find that's true for you, see if you can let yourself drop out of that mental world. Bring your attention back to your body and your breath. Allow yourself to settle down and see what's actually present in your experience, right now. Maybe you discover your body is agitated or feeling like it needs to defend itself. We live in a culture that encourages a nonstop fight-or-flight response, keeping people in chronic states of contraction and agitation.

By simply stopping and being present, you offer yourself the opportunity to return to homeostasis—the balancing of the nervous system, the healing of the body. You find out how to take care of yourself; you find out what you need. Maybe you change your diet or take a look at your habitual behaviors, some of which you may only just now be noticing.

We're learning and discovering all the time. For humans, life is always changing, so we're always finding our way, in every moment. But as we open into this awakened realm, we find a true sense of ease and of being guided—profoundly—into the infinite unknown. Now we can truly notice life and all its amazing details. We can really enjoy life as it is. We can find out why we're really here.

8.

Here to Be Here

Why are we here? We're here to *be* here—to *dissolve* into being here. Anything else is extra. So all you have to do is *notice* what's extra— notice where you're getting in your own way. You don't have to get rid of what's extra; you don't have to fix it; you don't even have to understand it. Just notice whatever in you *isn't* just being here, and allow yourself to *be here* with that too. I think you'll find that when *being here* is happening, there's a vibrancy, a sublime richness to your experience. *Enjoy* that richness.

As this verbal communication sinks in for you, you'll find that a subtler kind of communication is happening as well. In first encountering these teachings, you may notice a kind of resonance that touches that in you which is *already* awake. That radiant presence is fully alive in you right now, whether you are aware of it or not. The transmission of this teaching will seep in and, gradually, bring that aliveness to the forefront.

You may notice some side effects. You may find your sense of yourself expanding, becoming lighter, or your mind may become agitated; your emotions may become tumultuous. You may feel restlessness or anxiety. Often our bodies hold a lot of our pain, and as we begin to relax and open, that pain can come out.

So as this teaching resonates within you, be gentle with yourself. Be loving. Be forgiving and compassionate. The heart—your human heart—needs that compassion, as does your body, and your mind. They're all trying very hard to support you.

You know this already. You know what I'm talking about, and I'm sure you'll rediscover it over and over again as you learn to relax and allow yourself to *just be here*. Allow yourself to be profoundly nurtured and nourished by the love and unconditional acceptance that's inherent in the space of awareness. That's what heals us. That's what liberates us.

◇◇◇◇

Whether you realize it or not, you have many moments in your daily experience when *being here* is already happening—moments when there's nothing extra, when you're *not* in your own way, and you're very, very present. Something shifts, you drop out of your mental world, and suddenly you're fully in this moment, your senses vibrant and alive.

Maybe you're just walking along the sidewalk. You feel the wind on your face, and suddenly you're struck, transfixed by the sounds and feelings and motion swirling around you. Maybe you bite into some food that tastes amazing and have an incredible experience of flavors and smells and sensations. Or maybe you're simply absorbed by the quiet beauty of a flower or a sunset. In those moments there's a sense of connection, a vibrancy, and, even if for just an instant, no *you* to get in your own way. There's just presence, just aliveness.

In those moments you in a very real sense lose yourself, or at least the self you usually take yourself to be, and in losing yourself you paradoxically gain yourself in a much deeper way. You become fully engaged with your experience. You come *fully alive*.

◇◇◇◇

Anything you find yourself doing is an opportunity for that full engagement, and it can happen at any time, in any instant. So I invite you to make a practice of very, very gently cultivating those moments of awareness. In any moment, you can stop and check in with yourself, and ask:

Am I actually here right now?

Am I actually experiencing what's happening, or am I off in my head? Am I present for what's here in front of me, or am I worrying about the future or replaying the past?

If you're driving, really feel the steering wheel in your hands, the vibration of the car beneath your body, the momentum of your movement through space.

If you're walking, drop fully into that movement and feel your whole body—the soles of your feet rolling over the ground, your arms swinging back and forth, your breath moving in and out as you take one step after another.

Make a habit of checking in with yourself, reminding yourself to come back from wherever you've gone—back to your body, your feelings, your senses. Gradually you'll learn to interact with yourself in such a way that you become your own teacher, continually showing yourself how not to be in your own way, and how to be truly *here* in every moment of your life.

A moment of freedom is not just a taste of something you don't have; each moment of freedom *is* freedom itself! So treasure those moments, nurture them, and I think you'll find them happening more and more often.

◇◇◇◇

The desire to be liberated, to be free, is a beautiful longing, and we all share that. The good news is that it *will* happen. Full realization is your birthright, an amazing flowering built right into who and what you fundamentally are. That flowering doesn't require knowledge. It doesn't require perfection. All it requires is commitment and the willingness to show up, one hundred percent, with love, softness, and tenderness, and then naturally the heart will heal and the spirit will shine.

As this process unfolds, people are often surprised when they find that the mental and emotional patterns that have run them for their entire lives are suddenly just gone—that those patterns and tendencies have just fallen away. You don't have to fight and struggle to get rid of your karma, your compulsions, your negative trips. You only need to embrace yourself, accept and allow yourself. Then the true nature of what you are will emerge and come to the foreground, and in that moment a whole new life will begin.

So again, pay particular attention to what keeps you from being here, and keep bringing yourself back to this moment, over and over again. Even as you continue reading these words, notice how your mind periodically runs off into the past or the future. Without drawing any conclusions about that, without trying to figure out why it's happening or what it means, just notice it happening, and gently bring yourself back. Noticing, as simple as it might seem, is the doorway to this amazing movement of transformation.

How you give attention to what's happening is much more important than the actual things that are happening. The quality of your attention determines whether you'll be caught by your experience or able to allow it to flow through you like a passing breeze. Whether encountering pain, sorrow, or longing; rage, frustration, or confusion, simply *be the awareness* that perceives what's happening. *Be the space* that allows what's happening. And relax! You're not the one doing it. You don't have to make it happen.

Many people have the illusion that they're in control—that they're responsible for making progress and for becoming enlightened. I believed that for a long time. I was a good little spiritual achiever! But the truth is we're not responsible. We're not in control. Control has nothing to do with it. Expectations have nothing to do with it. Our beliefs and conclusions about the spiritual process have nothing to do with it.

So drop your ideas, let go of control, and let yourself simply *be this awareness* within which all that you perceive arises.

9.

Being, Not Doing

We're here to *be* here, but as I said, *being here* isn't actually something you can do. *Being here* isn't the result of effort. Rather, it's what's left when effort falls away. If you're *trying* to be here, there's still *someone* trying. The key is to drop that someone and drop the trying. Encourage your whole organism, your whole system, to let go of any effort, and then I think you'll find that *being here* happens by itself.

Being here is also not something that can be identified with, not something you can own or accomplish. Rather, it's simply what's happening when there's no one *trying* to be here—no one trying to get something, or get away from something, or understand something.

Take a look right now. Stop and *listen* into this moment. *Sense* into this moment. *Feel* into this moment. Notice any agitation, restlessness, or aversion: any kind of struggle in your mind or in your body. Are you distracted, having trouble paying attention? Is your mind spinning, pulling you off into the past or the future?

Now take a step back and notice the quality of that attention you've just brought to your experience. When you tune in like this, there's a kind of pointedness that arises, a sense of presence, focus, and aliveness. Recognize that aliveness—that's *being here*. Your surroundings may suddenly become more vivid: colors, sensations, energy shining brightly in your field of awareness. That's why we call it *awakening*. We're shocked awake, awestruck by the brilliance of this moment. So notice that awe. *Be* that awe.

After a time, you may find you've dropped back into sleep mode, or daydream mode, or analysis mode, off in the mind again. If that happens, don't judge yourself. Instead, with tenderness and forgiveness, just gently bring your attention back to this moment. Guide yourself to *be here*. At some point the imaginary self that really isn't here will vanish, and then you'll feel the heart connection, the love, the energy, the peacefulness—the *presence*.

You may also feel some agitation or discomfort. The expansion of awareness can be very pleasant, but it can also allow uncomfortable feelings to come to the forefront, pain or struggle you've been repressing or keeping at arm's length. If you find you're having a hard time, see if you can, as my mother would've said, "make nice on yourself." Offer yourself some comfort, some loving, tender compassion. In fact, stop reading and take a moment right now to make nice on yourself. When you come back, I think you'll feel the difference.

Notice also if you tend to externalize your energy. Do you project it out onto other people in the form of judgments? Bring all those projections back, and realize that everything that you see, feel, and sense is just a mirror—a mirror reflecting *you* back to yourself. Embrace that reflection. Bring it all back home. This is about inclusion, about *embracing everything*.

Now, I'm not suggesting that the conditional personal self should embrace everything. The embrace I'm talking about happens from the Big Heart, this vast field of awareness and presence. The same is true of compassion and forgiveness, which in their truest form come from that same Heart of Vastness. Of course they will also impact our human psychology, our human body, and our human heart, but it's important to distinguish clearly to avoid misunderstandings. Otherwise people can easily misinterpret these teachings and get caught up in yet another level of being and doing.

◇◇◇◇

I find it helpful to keep things simple, to as much as possible reduce things to the lowest common denominator of awareness itself. I want to help you become more and more intimate with that awareness and to begin to really trust how it reveals itself to you and how it guides you. The more you can allow awareness to come to the foreground, the more that trust will be present and the more you can relax and be guided.

It's been said that spiritual practice is like a cauldron, or a pressure cooker, and you're already cooking, already steeping in this awareness. You wouldn't be reading this book otherwise! You wouldn't have been attracted to it. You wouldn't have been ready. That's how far out this really is. We think we're guiding our own path, making a series of decisions that take us from one place to another, but that's not quite right. We're not doing it; *it's* doing us.

Of course, cooking is a hot process. Depending on what's been held in unconsciously, a lot can come to the surface—physical pain, emotional pain. This path is a cauldron of healing, and healing can be difficult. The healing process can be painful. But we're all cooking together! We're all in this together. So if you're struggling right now, hang in there. Be gentle with yourself. Be nice to yourself. See if you can give yourself a loving, nurturing hug.

◇◇◇◇

As I mentioned in the previous chapter, you may notice something that feels like a subtle energetic force field when encountering these teachings. If you are aware of that field, let yourself fall back into it. It can feel like you're floating on your back, like you're weightless. Or you might feel heavy; you might become aware of some energetic heaviness in your body that needs to be discharged.

As much as you can, stay outside of your mind. Don't think about this too much, and don't worry about understanding it or making sense of it intellectually. Relax and let the process develop as it needs to. Let what needs to happen, happen as it will. If your mind begins spinning out of control, then just redirect your attention into your breath, into the bodily sensations that are arising in the field of your awareness. As best you can, let the thoughts play out and pass on their own. You may find that in even considering that idea, your relationship to your thoughts begins to shift in an entirely new direction.

10.

So What *Can* I Do?

Often people say to me, "I know I'm not supposed to do anything, but there must be *something* I can do!" Or, "I know I'm not supposed to try to understand this, but can't I at least understand it a little bit?"

I have to tell you that of the people I've been close to who are what I would call "awakened," each and every one would readily admit that they are basically clueless—that they have no idea what's actually going on! Who they are and where they live from has nothing to do with knowing or with conventional understanding, but emerges spontaneously from the vastness and freedom of *not knowing.*

Reality is unknowable. It's unexplainable. Although it might initially seem frightening to think you can never really know anything, as you really let that in, I think you'll find it's actually an enormous relief. Gradually you'll stop relying on your mind and instead learn to trust in your body and your heart. Now you don't have to figure out the reasons and causes of what's happening. You don't need to know what any of it means. You can just let yourself be human, and respond in whatever way the moment calls for.

Again, that's not to say our minds are useless. Sometimes you need to figure things out on a practical level—how to get somewhere, or install some software, or organize your finances—and the mind is obviously a fantastic tool for addressing those kinds of practical issues. The problems arise when we use our minds to try to advance ourselves spiritually. We imagine that through analysis and intellectual understanding, we'll progress on the path, but ironically, in that very effort, we prevent our own liberation.

So drop out of the mind. Find the natural flow of emotion, and let it move through you without worrying about what it "means" or why it's happening. As you bring careful, gentle attention to even the challenging aspects of your human experience—whether that's pain in your body, worry in your mind, or even long-held trauma— you'll find that things can heal. Pain you thought would be there forever might suddenly dissolve. But even if that doesn't happen, by giving yourself permission simply to be human, you'll find a natural ease of being that will allow you to be relaxed and fundamentally happy regardless of your circumstances or challenges.

◇◇◇◇

I crave that ease, but every time I get close to it, something happens that seems to be out of my control, and then the peace is gone.

It sounds like you're trying to make peace happen. But the truth is you can't intentionally move toward ease. All you can do is bring awareness to where you *actually are* in this moment. Any attempt to *get* peace will only create tension internally, subtly pushing that peace away.

But don't worry about that right now. In *this* moment, you're here. You're present. Can you let yourself *just* be here? Notice if you're trying to get something from this moment, trying to make it a certain way, or even trying to hold on to something about it that you like. Now take a step back, and just *notice* that trying. *That's* where you want to put your attention.

Ironically, if you focus on the ease, you'll actually get caught up in the trying. You'll be *identified* with the trying. So simply *notice* the trying, and bring awareness to the *one* who is trying—the limited, human person who's desperate for that ease and is trying so hard to get it. There's no blame for that, no judgment. You're human, and that's just how humans are conditioned to operate. But if you can bring that dynamic into consciousness, you'll find it will begin to dissolve by itself.

46

◇◇◇◇

I get so angry with myself because I can't seem to get this. I feel responsible for my own suffering.

Again, no blame. Be gentle with yourself. If you find yourself getting frustrated, try offering yourself a little forgiveness, a little compassion. If that's difficult, then try it the other way around. Talk to yourself. Ask yourself for forgiveness. "I'm sorry. I'm sorry I'm so angry, destructive, frustrated. Please forgive me." That will help your heart soften and open.

You don't want to live at war with yourself, do you? So make peace. Be nice to yourself. Have some compassion for your own suffering. See how that works.

The quality of wanting has a forward motion to it. And that's fine! No blame, no judgment. But that forward motion can prevent us from being conscious of this presence, this ease that's always available to us if we're available to it. As soon as you let go and really drop into being here, the flower of that ease will bloom naturally.

◇◇◇◇

The process of awakening and transformation is not within your control. It's not yours *to* control. It's going to happen the way it's going to happen, and you're not going to be in the driver's seat. So realize that the one who wants to control just wants to be safe and secure, and offer that one some compassion. Offer yourself permission to be as you are, and then your heart can release its fear. That's what the heart wants, what it truly yearns for.

So if you find yourself compulsively trying to control your experience, don't worry too much about it. That part of you that wants to be in control, however compulsive or compromised it may be, can nevertheless guide you on the path. As you bring gentle awareness to that struggling part, you bring awareness to its underlying condition or conflicts, and now you see where to put your energy. So trust that awareness. Let it lead you, and let it show you the way.

11.

Accepting What Is

Just being here, there's a space of availability, of openness. In our daily lives we can get so wound up that even when we finally have the space to listen, we may still not hear. Usually we're so busy getting somewhere that we don't taste the flavor of *right now*.

That's not to say that flavor will always be pleasant! Sometimes the flavor of right now is exhaustion, or discomfort; or grief, wanting, or confusion. But openness allows for *whatever* is happening now, without getting caught in what it means, without trying to change it. It also allows noticing when our mind is already habitually trying to change or fix our experience. When we bring attention to that subtle fighting, the subtle resistance of *trying to change things*, then space appears around that dynamic, and instantly its power is lessened.

Whatever is happening, you can always step back, just a bit, and view the situation from the perspective of awareness. Notice how it *actually is* in this moment, rather than trying to make it how you want it to be. When all else fails, try acceptance!

I don't mean acceptance as a kind of psychological method, where you apply a new mental frame or filter that says things are good now. Rather, I invite you to perceive from beyond the thinking mind, directly from spaciousness. Simply perceive things as they *actually are*, directly from awareness itself. You *are* that awareness, and acceptance is your fundamental nature. Just as the ocean allows whatever is in it to be there, whether that's sea creatures, plankton, or garbage, awareness inherently allows whatever is present simply to pass through its spacious field.

That's not to say you don't participate in life, that you don't take action as needed. True acceptance does not equal resignation or putting up with things that are not okay. When we truly wake up, we find we can act, participate, contribute, and serve in ways we couldn't have imagined before. We're able to go right into the storm, right into the fire, without hesitation. We take whatever action is needed, do what needs to be done.

In Zen they say "Take care of what's in front of you." That doesn't mean "Be a good person." Of course it might show up that way, but the intent is different. When you're truly awake, and truly integrated, you *are* a good person. That doesn't mean you'll always make perfect decisions or that you'll never make mistakes, but your actions will arise from the heart, from the compassionate space of openness.

Of course not everyone who wakes up to some extent does become truly integrated. Some people gain access to the energy of awakening and develop powerful charisma, but never do the important work of honestly facing their dark side and their human limitations. This can be problematic (to put it mildly) for the people who approach them as students. If you've followed the history of spirituality in the West over the past several decades, I'm sure you know exactly what I'm talking about.

So it's immensely important that nothing in us be denied, nothing be ignored or glossed over. We have to reclaim *all* of ourselves, even the parts we'd rather not deal with, in order to blossom fully as complete human beings. I often say that there's really no spiritual work to be done, but only human work. When you find out *how* to do that human work—how to relax into your humanity and allow it to be exactly as it is—then your heart naturally opens, and your spirit naturally shines.

Awakening is completely natural, but we, through our wound-edness and conditioning, have fallen from that natural grace. We've lost touch with what we really are. But at the same time we *know* that grace and that instinctive knowledge are the source of the deep longing that brings us here to this path, and show us the inner guidance system that's calling us home.

12.

Finding the Guidance System

How do you find your way back to the source of being? How do you get in touch with that inner guidance system? What do I even mean by "inner guidance system"?

To offer a physical analogy, your body has a natural balance system that allows you to walk or run without falling over. You don't need to think about it—when you stumble, you don't pause to consider whether you've lost your balance and decide what to do about it. You know you're falling, and you react immediately. You are in a sense "guided" by this system to react immediately and try to remain upright. Similarly, we have a kind of psychic balance system that is always available to us. Its feedback is much more subtle, though, and we need to learn to recognize the guidance it offers.

The field of transmission can help you become attuned to that guidance, making it available on a more conscious level as you learn to relax into new levels of sensitivity. You might experience this initially as a kind of increased vulnerability, which can feel uncomfortable at first. Often the experience of opening or letting go can feel like a loss of control. We have a primal need to be in control—to protect ourselves, to survive. Our compulsion to understand and to make meaning of our experience is an extension of this survival impulse.

But the guidance system I'm talking about is beyond meaning, beyond understanding. It's like a force of nature that flows through us. So notice that force. One way to facilitate that noticing is to become aware of your senses, to open fully to sensation. Try it right now. See if you can let your mind be in the background somewhere, out of the way of what's arising right now, and give your attention to even the subtlest of sensations that are arising.

Any sensation that's present—visual, kinesthetic, auditory— can be a doorway to the infinite, a message from the guidance system within. Anything you surrender your attention to has the power to guide you back home. But as I've said, it's not simply *that* you give attention to what's happening, but *how* you give attention that's important. If you direct your attention in a way that is forced, that will only create further contraction.

So as you shift your attention to sensation, be aware of the quality of that attention. Is it forced—is it creating more tension in your body or mind? Or is it relaxed, open, restful? You might also ask yourself: *Who* is paying attention? If you have a strong sense of being the person who is observing, of *doing* this whole "attention to sensations" thing, then you're not really diving in all the way yet.

A common Zen instruction says "Let your mind drop into your breath." Let go of thinking about what you're doing, of being someone who *is* doing. Allow yourself to vanish into your experience. Awakening is the great disappearing act! So let yourself disappear. Dive fully into *right now*.

If there's resistance, still someone who is trying or struggling, then no worries, and no blame. You can only start right where you actually are. So take a breath, then let it out, relaxing your shoulders, your chest, your belly. Try a few more breaths, really allowing yourself to relax. Now express where you're really at, right now, into the space of awareness: "I'm struggling right now. I'm having a hard time." Let that expression resonate in the space, in the silence. See if you can notice the stillness within the struggle—the space within which the struggle arises. Open to that stillness. Rest in that space.

I often recommend to people that they make a point of spending at least some time in openness every day. For some that might mean taking up a regular, formal sitting practice, but it could also mean just taking a moment now and then to stop, and rest, and allow yourself to reconnect with that stillness right in the midst of whatever else might be happening for you.

I've already suggested a few ways to cultivate those moments, but as you deepen in this process, you'll notice that, more and more, those moments of awareness happen on their own. At any time, whatever you're doing, you might suddenly find that the self you've always taken yourself to be has dropped away, and you're *just here* without it. So notice those moments as they come, and enjoy them. Surrender to them. Treasure them.

◇◇◇◇

If you want to remember anything I've said in this book, make it this: *Just be right here.* Give yourself permission to be right here. Whatever it takes to be right here—forgiveness, compassion, patience, tenderness—allow yourself to receive it, and then really listen to the teaching in the sound of silence, in the alive stillness.

Awakening happens by itself. The only thing we're really learning here is how to *allow* it to happen. Take a moment to really let that in. I think you'll find it lifts the burden of being responsible for your spiritual progress from your shoulders, giving you a whole different perspective on what responsibility really means. Just bringing awareness to *what is*, allowing it to be as it is in the field of awareness, you might say that's a kind of effortless responsibility, effortless grace.

The secret is just discovering what *being awareness* is, what *being presence* is—and then rediscovering it over and over and over again. That's the perspective that allows awakening to happen. Any attempt to grasp for or hold on to awakening only obscures it. As human beings we're so programmed to survive, to seek comfort and avoid pain, and so it's difficult for us to trust that the process is happening and to let that awareness take us.

But eventually we do begin to learn, and gradually we realize that this presence has a kind of force field, and every cell in our body can dissolve into that field. Enlightenment is the enlivening of the body, the enlivening of the mind—and vibrant aliveness of *being*.

13.

Surrender

The process of realization is really about learning to communicate with the infinite—which is mostly just learning to listen. You may be familiar with the old Christian prayer, "Not my will, but Thine be done." From our perspective that prayer is an invitation to really listen, to realize that there's more to life than this little box called "you" with its dramas and its history and future. Life is infinite. We are infinite.

Even when life is painful, that too is a communication. We may not want the pain or discomfort—or the grief, the sadness, the fear, the anger—but it's there for a reason. It's a communication. So we learn to *receive* that communication.

At first this is as simple as just listening to feelings, feeling sensations, and this may seem very individual, very particular to ourselves. But what initially feels so personal ultimately leads to the *unwinding* of the personal—to the dissolution of the separate self. This can be frightening at first. Often people begin opening up, but then find themselves quickly putting the brakes on! In my own case, I would get deeper and deeper into awareness, but then find myself contracting again as my instinctive fear of unwinding took hold.

The problem was that I was still *somebody*, a person with an agenda of getting myself deeper and deeper into awareness. So I kept thinking, *Well, I just need more awareness, more presence,* and I would try harder, pushing myself to be more aware, more present. But as things got more intense, there would be a stopping, a kind of clamping down of my system. I would think it was my fault: *I stopped it again!* I'd think I wasn't good enough, focused enough, disciplined enough—all those ridiculous self-judgments.

But eventually there was a moment—I remember it well—when somehow I just surrendered, simply and naturally, and that was the end of it. The fear didn't come up anymore. The stopping stopped! There was no more clamping down on the infinite. But it wasn't the result of some decision I made to stop clamping down. It wasn't the result of effort at all. Rather, it was a falling away of effort. When I was finally ready, surrender happened by itself.

Until you reach that point of readiness, though, it's completely normal and natural to experience the cycle of opening and then resisting again. So relax, let it happen, and most importantly, don't worry about it! The conditioned self is afraid—afraid of letting go, of being out of control, of going crazy, of not existing anymore, but that's just the natural instinct of the human organism to protect itself and survive. Just know that when you're ready, you'll go all the way. Opening will happen by itself.

If you can just *be* this awareness, be this presence, and not think about it, that's enough. The rest will take care of itself. You will be guided. You will be transformed. In fact, you already have been; you *always* have been. You are already that which you seek. All that's necessary is to allow the dropping away of the veil that prevents you from perceiving it.

The dissolving of that veil is what's called transformation. It might appear to be change, great change, but it's really just an uncovering, a revealing of what's always been here. So we're not getting somewhere, or gaining something, or becoming someone new. We're simply letting go of what's been in the way of our seeing and allowing ourselves to perceive the truth of who and what we already very naturally are.

14.

Meditation: Stillness and Balance

As you become more comfortable over time with your sitting practice, you might explore allowing yourself to be very, very still. I don't mean the kind of rigid stillness in which you exert effort to prevent yourself from moving; rather, I mean a deep, relaxed stillness that contains no effort whatsoever. You're not still in the sense of being controlled, but more in the sense of being *completely balanced*. Even if you feel imbalanced—maybe your energy is all over the place or you feel physically off in some way—see if you can remain still and really tune in to that feeling of not being balanced.

I spent most of my twenties as a monk in a Zen monastery, where I spent probably the majority of my time meditating for many years. There were periods, sitting there quietly, when I would feel like my body was completely contorted, as if I were twisted way over to one side. But when I actually looked down at myself I would realize that I wasn't contorted at all, that in fact I was sitting perfectly upright despite how strange my body felt. Since I didn't have any other choice—I was in a monastery, observing a monastic schedule—I got to have the experience of letting that feeling be, which was very, very interesting.

Sometimes you just need to let yourself be however you happen to be right now—without trying to fix it, without exerting effort to shift yourself to some better way of being. When you can open to presence, when you are able to tune in in that way, then rest as that presence. But at other times when you find that presence doesn't seem to be available, then just listen in to your body—to what you're sensing, what you're feeling, to the movement of your breath.

See if you can drop out of your head, out of your thinking, and guide yourself back into your body, into your breath, into sensing, feeling. You may notice, as you tune in, that a deep stillness is already present. You *are* that stillness, you *are* that presence, and as over time that becomes more obvious, you'll find yourself always returning to it regardless of what circumstances you find yourself in.

So there's a kind of effortless stillness that's very important, and in that stillness the shift into *being presence* can happen in any moment. Experiencing that shift can be very powerful. Things begin to open, and heal, and transform. Your body becomes a kind of hothouse and a very powerful laboratory for transformation.

So when we sit, quietly tuning in to the body, things begin to happen, things shift. There can be a kind of transitional period; you may feel heavy, or sluggish, or sleepy, or distracted. But at a certain point, something just sort of comes together. The body relaxes and becomes more aware, more sensitive. Attention becomes very precise, very subtle, and there's a brightness, a vividness of experience that emerges. It could be described as openness, receptivity, availability—or freshness. That freshness lets you know the instrument is tuned.

So what gets in the way of that? What prevents us from resting that way all the time? Usually what gets in the way is what we want and what we don't want—that is, the mind's ongoing struggle with the way things are. Most people find their mind to be problematic.

So how does the mind become free? How does our thinking mind become our ally? One of the easiest ways to liberate the mind is to question what you believe, question the stories you're telling yourself. Are they true? And when some story is running through your mind, notice what kind of impact it has on the body. Does the body feel restricted? Is there some physical contraction in response to the story? And notice the impact on your feelings: Does it make you feel more alienated, more separate? By inquiring in this way, you begin to really understand the effect of thinking on the nervous system and on the quality of conscious experience.

The tricky part is to notice what's happening, but without judging it or trying to control it. That's when you'll encounter the real learning curve. As you bring attention to what's happening, whether it's a contraction or reaction, the key insight is not that you can't stop the reaction, but that you can simply be the spacious awareness that perceives it. *That* is the springboard into awakening—into being awareness, rather than being identified as a reactive, defensive, contracted, separate, alienated person.

Conceptually, it's profoundly simple. But it requires walking the walk, not just talking the talk. We have to step out of our paradigms and beliefs and actually wake up to *not knowing* right now. Not knowing, but instead listening, seeing, feeling. Surrendering, being guided. Getting out of our own way. It takes courage, no doubt about that, and often it also takes hitting bottom when you find that whatever you've been trying to do just isn't working anymore. As the old saying goes, if the only tool you have is a hammer, you tend to treat all your problems as if they're nails. Just hit it harder, right? That might make you feel like you're getting somewhere, but I can attest from long-term experience that it doesn't work!

Awakening is our natural condition. If it's not foreground right now, it's just under layers of stuff. That's all. So you don't have to get it; you don't have to achieve it. All you have to do is relax and forgive yourself. Have compassion for whatever the condition is or the circumstances are. And watch awareness grow; watch it bloom; watch it expand and deepen.

15.

The Natural Force of Awakening

Awakening is completely natural, a force of nature. Often we think we need to accomplish awakening—that we need to understand some teaching, or do some practice correctly to make it happen. Or *not do* it, as the case may be—we may find ourselves trying to "do" non-doing, putting a lot of effort into no-effort! But awakening happens by itself, outside of all our struggles. Like gravity. Like birth. Like the movement of the planet.

Awakening is a force of nature, and it's *ongoing*. However far we "advance" on the so-called path, awakening continues. People often think of awakening as a destination, a place they'll have arrived where they'll think, *I have now awakened!* You may imagine you'll have a linear sense of arriving, of having gotten somewhere you weren't before. Our minds and language tend to support that kind of conceptual thinking. But awakening is not an endpoint. It's a movement, and it's ongoing.

Another way to describe awakening is, of course, *being*. As I've said, *being* is simply allowing what's already happening—that is, *seeing what's real*, and allowing it to be what it is. *Being* is free of the many perceptual filters of the personal self that stand between us and our experience. Despite those filters, we can always embrace *being*, in any moment. All that's required is bringing awareness to that filtering process.

Of course what I'm really pointing to once again is how our *identities* interfere with our ability to experience our lives directly. Our identities are, in a very real sense, *made of* those perceptual filters. To see past them is to penetrate the veil of illusion that identity creates and to begin instead to live in the immediacy of *what is*.

The most difficult filter to see through is, of course, *knowing*. Our minds really, really want to know. It's what they're designed for—to analyze and understand our experience so they can protect us and keep us alive. Of course that's a very important function, and our minds are very useful on a practical level. We do need to feed ourselves, find shelter, avoid stepping in front of buses, and so on.

But in the spiritual realm, that kind of knowing is much less useful. Knowing can be an occlusion—it can be very dense, almost opaque—and since it's been our primary survival strategy throughout our lives, knowing can also be very difficult to let go of. But eventually you get to a point where even knowing drops away. Now there's no longer anything between you and what's *actually happening*, right here, in this moment.

When finally we're *just here*, there's an intimacy, a closeness with our experience. It can be a little scary, a little vulnerable, especially at first. We're still a human organism that wants to feel like it's safe, wants to know it's not going to be hurt. And of course if we have a memory of being hurt, which most of us do to one extent or another, then being vulnerable can feel more than a little threatening. How can we know it's safe?

Feelings of fear and insecurity are very common as the filters begin to dissolve, but as you gradually allow yourself to relax more and more into presence and being, those dynamics begin to settle into a new balance. You realize that awakening is not just something that is happening to you, but actually *what you already are*, and as awakening progresses further, there's a deepening into that awareness. Now vulnerability is not so threatening anymore—in fact, it's a big relief! A natural trust emerges, and a deeper letting go happens by itself.

You can't force this process. The parts of you that have been damaged, that need healing, may take time to unwind and integrate. That's why it's also important to bring in compassion and forgiveness, and gratitude, and love! So much of this process is really an opening of the heart and a letting go of your ideas about how it will unfold. If you can relinquish your ideas of spiritual progress—dropping the filters of expectation: "Am I here yet? Is this it? How much longer?"—then you can allow the human process to continue as it needs to.

Often people become quite radiant and expanded, very far along the path, you might say, but then suddenly some very difficult psychological or emotional material emerges, something that was never consciously processed. As we begin to loosen up internally, things we've repressed or avoided dealing with in ourselves can become unavoidable.

I often say that after the initial awakening comes the *rude awakening*, and it can be quite a shock. I'll have more to say about this later, but for now, just understand that it's not a problem. In fact, it's a sign of progress! As long as you understand that the "rude awakening" is simply part of the process, you can allow it to happen as it needs to. You can welcome those painful parts of yourself back into your heart. They need your love and acceptance, your forgiveness and gratitude—and then they can relax, and come home, and take their places as parts of a fuller, more integrated self.

◇◇◇◇

So awakening is a natural force, and it's ongoing, which is great news! That means you're not doing it, and you're therefore not responsible for it. You're free of that responsibility. So what *is* your role in the process? What can you do to help it along? The answer is, mostly, be here for the show! Be very, very attentive, 100 percent present for your own experience. As I often say, you're already paying rent, so you may as well move in!

There's also a kind of self-care that's very important. Too often on the spiritual path, people deny themselves in ways that are not healthy. They may worry that by tending to their human-level needs, they're not being "spiritual" enough, or that they're strengthening or reifying the separate self. But I'm here to tell you that loving, tender care for yourself while on the spiritual path is not only possible, but essential, particularly as the awakening process really gets under way.

But you won't have to try too hard even at taking care of yourself. As you realize more and more that what you truly are is this *presence*, this beautiful energy that animates the body and the mind alike, then naturally the spirit wants to care for the human. Our humanness doesn't need to be transcended; it needs to be embraced, allowed, and given full permission to be exactly what it is.

One of my personal commitments is to do what I can to make this path a lot lighter—and a lot funnier! Spirituality has traditionally been so serious, so heavy. I honor the path and the commitment, obviously; I wouldn't be doing this otherwise. But I think we can really find ease in it and lightness in it, rather than heaviness and seriousness. And pleasure! Don't forget pleasure. We're human beings. We're sentient. We feel, and we prefer to feel good! Feeling light, relaxed, and happy can only help, only facilitate and encourage this process of deepening.

Enlightenment is always here. Everything is a part of it. So see if you can let yourself be a part of it too. Find your ease in being—right here, right now. See what in you can be released, surrendered, let go. Whether there's some contraction in the body or some struggle in the mind, some feeling that's trying to move, or some fear holding you back, just bring gentle attention to whatever's happening. That's all you need to do. Find out how to *allow* what's happening so the quality of your attention doesn't interfere with it. If there's no interference, then there's no effort, no doing.

As effort drops away and knowing drops away, and that deep trust permeates your being, you begin to see that everything in your experience, and every*one* in your experience, is actually a mirror—is actually you yourself! When you really understand that—when that really begins to sink in—wow! Your heart blasts wide open.

16.

Questions That Release You

Although I've written a lot of words in this book, I want to emphasize again that my intention is not to offer concepts for you to understand or beliefs for you to adopt. At best, these words are pointers or suggestions to help you find out how to allow the natural force of awakening to unfold on its own.

When you look at a flower, you probably don't think, *How did it do that? How did it bloom? How did it blossom?* Yet often we ask essentially those same questions when we talk about awakening: *How do we become free? What can we do to make it happen?* Of course it's fine, and completely understandable, to ask those questions. But if instead of trying to answer the questions, you can instead *feel* the questions— feel the desire or longing behind them, that energy from which they arise—you may find that the questions are more useful than any answers you might find.

Again, awakening is a natural force, and questions like these are an opportunity, an invitation, to allow that force to work through you and transform you. To truly understand the energy of the questions is to shift your essential sense of who you are from the limited person you've always taken yourself to be, with a history and personality, to the *space of being* within which the story of that person has unfolded.

So go ahead and ask the questions, but instead of trying to answer them—trying to figure them out, trying to understand them—just let the questions settle. Sit with the questions. Rest in the questions. Rest *as* the questions. And notice the *space* within which the questions arise—the space of listening. The space of *being*.

Now take a step back and allow yourself to rest *as* that space of being—without tension, without resistance. Open fully to what's arising in the field of your awareness. Let yourself just be available so that you're not pushing against your experience or fighting it. With tenderness, compassion, and patience, allow yourself to *just be here.*

◇◇◇◇

Asking yourself questions can be useful in other ways. If you're caught up in struggle and you find yourself in a space of discomfort or confusion, the mind's natural desire to know, to question, and to figure things out can be made use of. You can talk to yourself, and ask: "*Who* is uncomfortable or confused? Who doesn't want to feel that way? And what *is* this wanting, or this *not* wanting?"

Now, *just* asking questions isn't really enough on its own. You have to let yourself feel the energy behind each question—really feel, for instance, that wanting to be in control. But often you can get there through questioning. Asking yourself these kinds of questions can help you redirect your attention and open you to exploring a different kind of relationship with your experience.

These exact questions may or may not resonate for you, and that's fine! As I've said, I'm not here to offer you a formula or a rigid "way" to follow. I'm here to offer pointers, gentle suggestions that will help you find your *own* way. So find the questions that release you, that relax you, and that allow opening to happen.

◇◇◇◇

Your questions to yourself don't always have to be weighty and spiritual. You might simply ask, for instance, "Have I been nice to myself today?" That may not seem like a very "spiritual" sort of question, but when you're nice to yourself, your "self" tends to relax and open up a bit, and is just that much more willing to let go of control. It may eventually dissolve and not even be there at all. When the self dissolves, what's left is just love. Just openness.

So if you find yourself struggling, be kind to yourself. Give yourself some compassion, some gentleness. Most of us have to relearn that because we're really hard on ourselves. We're always judging, comparing, regretting, looking back, looking forward. It's no wonder we often feel alone or abandoned, because so many of us are just not in the habit of taking care of ourselves.

So get in that habit. Cultivate a practice of periodically checking in with yourself, of giving yourself a bit of self-care. You might do it right now. Take a moment and bring your attention back into your breath, into your body. Feel into where you're at in this moment—your feelings, your desires, or your aversions or confusion if those are present. Let yourself settle. Let awareness open.

Opening is the movement of your true nature. It doesn't have to be difficult. It doesn't even have to be a big deal! It can be as simple as getting in a hot bath and relaxing. Letting yourself breathe. Gradually your body will learn to be more relaxed, to let go of its defensiveness, its fear of being hurt or being taken advantage of, or just being unloved or unfulfilled.

When you take care of yourself, even in the smallest ways, you cultivate a subtle kind of healing. Even taking a brief moment to tune in, as you did just now, is very deep healing work, and in that healing, the heart and the spirit will merge and flourish. You don't have to understand how to have an open heart. You don't have to figure out how to be loving. When that blossom is ready, it will bloom.

Of course it's not always easy to be kind to yourself. You may not always feel loving. But whatever you're feeling, whatever's pushing your buttons, *that's* where to bring your attention. That's where the juice is, the place where transformation is possible. So instead of running away from your buttons being pushed, or trying to avoid them being pushed, take a step back and just *notice* that they're being pushed. Be the space within which that "button-pushing" happens.

If you're caught in your mind and it's flying or spinning off some-where, don't worry too much about it. There's probably just some kind of clearing going on, some kind of purging, and that's okay! Your mind is doing the best it can. Don't fight it, and don't blame it. Just let there be a little voice in there with it that reminds you to bring yourself back: back here to your breath, to your body, to your feelings.

Freedom is your natural state of being. If you can just sense this space, this energy, this presence, and then give yourself fully to that, surrender into that, then liberation and the fullness of life will be your condition, regardless of circumstance or any personal limitations you might have.

17.

The Hallmark of Intimacy

Again, awakening is the natural movement of this life. The particular transition we usually call "awakening," or enlightenment, or realization, is simply recognizing that movement, discovering it—and *being* it. Awakening is beyond all conceptualization, beyond all interpretation, and yet it is the very essence of our moment-to-moment experience. When conceptualization drops away, awakening is already *right here*.

The question is really how to allow that *dropping away* to happen: Why hasn't it already happened? What's preventing it? What's holding on? As you deepen in this process, what you'll find is that holding, that resistance, is anchored in the body as a kind of subtle contraction you are probably not even consciously aware of.

We've been conditioned to hold ourselves in, to behave properly, and to act like good little girls and boys. We have human needs to belong, and so we're socialized and acculturated accordingly. We learn to be repressed, to "keep it together"—that is, to maintain our *identities*.

Identity is that "keeping it together"—the holding together of the bundle of beliefs that make up your limited, separate self, which also manifests as that subtle physical contraction in the body. Relaxing that contraction—and releasing the energy bound up in it—requires that we first become aware of it, that we bring that contraction into consciousness and recognize how it affects our experience.

That's why so many traditional spiritual instructions—meditation, breathing exercises, movement practices—direct us out of thinking and into breathing, into sensing, into connecting more deeply with the experience of our physical bodies. Tuning in to our bodies in this way opens us to a more kinesthetic consciousness, from the perspective of which the contraction of the self becomes much more obvious. As we inquire more deeply, it also opens us to an energetic perception that goes beyond the seeming boundaries of this body.

When people begin to awaken, they can experience intense energetic changes, all kinds of energies blowing through their systems, and what's been held in and locked down can really begin to wake up and move. These kinds of "spiritual fireworks" can really grab your attention, and it's easy to get caught up in that process and think awakening is all about having some fire hose of energy rushing through you at all times. But like everything else, that phase passes eventually. Your channels clear, and then you're just open, relaxed, available.

I sometimes speak of this openness as *intimacy*. It's a nearness, a closeness, a deep enmeshment with our experience. It's akin to human empathy, when you literally feel someone else's experience, where your heart is one with theirs. I recently heard a mother talking about her daughter. She said it was like her heart was running around in another body. What awakening shows us is that our heart is everyone's heart; our heart is the heart of everything.

Accessing this intimacy requires *allowing vulnerability*. It requires the willingness to not be in control; to be open, receptive; to *not know* what's happening; to not even know who you are. You have to allow yourself to be unwound, released. You have to allow your limited personal self to dissolve.

Vulnerability is the hallmark of intimacy, and intimacy emerges naturally in the absence of the personal self. We are this oneness being itself, deepening into itself, expanding into itself, and loving itself. Awakening is not a singular event; rather, it's a movement, a process, a happening—not enlighten*ment*, but enlighten*ing*. It's endless movement, endless illumination. *That's* intimacy. That's the one mind, the one heart, that we all share.

So welcome yourself to let go, right now. Surrender into vulnerability and openness, and whatever needs to unravel or unwind or release from your body or your heart, invite it to let go. Because it will!

Sometimes people encounter these kinds of teachings and find themselves feeling uncomfortable. They don't initially realize they've entered a kind of hothouse, a spiritual pressure cooker, and they may find they want to run out the door. But you don't want to be a half-baked potato. You want to go all the way! In fact, you don't even have the option of going only halfway. Once you're on this path, you're committed. You can try to go backward, but the potato will always find its way back to the oven.

The good news is that realization is effortless. It's not a doing, not an accomplishment. It's not an attainment. Rather, it's a deep discovery. So you sit, and welcome what's happening right now—even if what's happening is resistance, or arguing, or complaining. Kvetching! Longing. Welcome what is, *whatever* it is. Trust that this light and energy and presence will reveal itself when it's time—whenever that is. It can't be orchestrated; it can't be constructed; it can't be engineered. It can't be understood! But it can, without a doubt, be *realized* and fully embodied.

Then you can finally live your life fully, however and whatever your life is. On the surface everything might be exactly the same, but in the richness of presence, you will have been transformed.

18.

Suggestions for Transformation

.

Can you *locate* awareness? If you try, you'll notice that awareness is no place in particular, and yet it's everywhere. It's everything that is. It's what *we* are. So the underlying question is, what *is* this awareness? Following are some suggestions that I think might be helpful toward this inquiry, some hints for allowing understanding to emerge.

I invite you to

listen without thinking,

see without identifying,

feel without interpreting,

sense without resisting, and

allow thoughts without believing them.

Try these instructions out, one at a time. As always, don't push yourself or try too hard. Just go through them in the most relaxed way you can. If one doesn't make sense to you, skip to the next. If none of them make sense, skip them all! As always, this is not about handing you a way to follow, but about helping you find your own way.

◇◇◇◇

Listen without thinking. Sound is such an ongoing, accessible, ever-present reality, all around us at all times. So I invite you to *just listen,* without thinking about what you're hearing—without naming what you're hearing, or analyzing it, or judging it. Let sound simply be what it is, and notice the silence beneath the sound. Let yourself *be* that silence within which sound arises.

In any moment, you can listen without thinking—dropping the mind, becoming the space of listening. You'll know you're on the right track when you feel your awareness expanding as the space of listening opens up. You'll find yourself dropping into a scintillating attentiveness that is completely free of tension, a kind of radiant balance point.

See without identifying. The field of vision is a very vulnerable and receptive realm, but so often we miss what's right in front of us as our mind compulsively labels everything we see. We allow our expectations and beliefs to shape our experience. So drop the filters of the mind, drop your expectations, your assumptions and beliefs, and allow yourself simply to see what is arising in your visual field—without labeling it, without interpreting it, and without believing anything about it. You may notice a new vividness, a vibrancy that is suddenly quite prominent. If you can relax into that vividness and allow yourself to really go with it, you'll find that your experience opens up in ways you wouldn't have expected.

Feel without interpreting. So often we allow ourselves to be caught up in our feelings—in their meaning, in the story and history behind them, and so on. There's definitely a place for that; in the proper context, delving into our feelings in that way can be very helpful. But when cultivating awareness, the mental content we associate with our feelings can be a real distraction. So I invite you instead simply to feel what you're feeling, without figuring it out, without investing your feelings with meaning. Drop the conceptual frame around your feelings and just notice them as energy, as movement, as sensations. You'll find an openness, a space around your feelings that you may not have noticed before.

That space, that openness, is the sign from your internal guidance system that you're headed in the right direction. It's a kind of psychic biofeedback, you might say; shifting your attention, you may suddenly feel a lot more relaxed, or open, or peaceful. You no longer feel like you need to get somewhere, or get something, or figure something out. There's just a kind of open, easy settledness, an ease of being. Follow that ease, and allow it to lead you home.

Sense without resisting. Often we resist what we sense kinesthetically in our bodies. We may encounter sensations we'd rather not be having, maybe some pain or tension. This creates a cycle of reactive feelings in the mind—the *not wanting* the pain and maybe some beating ourselves up for having the pain in the first place—which creates more tension in the body and often more pain. So I invite you to, as best you can, relax your body and simply sense. Simply allow whatever sensations appear in your body to arise in the space of awareness.

Allow thoughts without believing them. Our minds are amazing manifestations of the creative emergence of this universe. They can obviously do incredible things, and yet they can cause us a lot of suffering if we take our thoughts to be the complete truth of reality. So while it might be challenging at first, see if you can let your thoughts simply arise in your mind without believing them. You'll know you're believing your thoughts if you find that there's a charge on them. If you're believing your thoughts and they're challenged from outside, you'll become reactive and find yourself defending a position—that is, holding on to an *identity*.

There's nothing wrong with thought in and of itself; thoughts, concepts, and even beliefs can be useful and functional so long as we don't invest our identity in them. Thoughts, when arising from and imbued with awareness, can be deeply inspirational, even enlightening. As I often say, it's okay to have beliefs—as long as you don't believe them! It's not like we're throwing away thought. We're just returning the mind to its rightful place as a supportive ally, transforming it from something that enslaves us to something that supports our ongoing liberation.

◇◇◇◇

Any of these instructions, applied with curiosity and openness, may produce in you a moment of freedom, and as I've said, even the briefest moment of freedom *is* true freedom! A taste of the truth, even a momentary glimpse of the truth, *is* the truth. If it slips away again, no blame and no worries. You haven't lost anything. Freedom is your nature. You can't lose that which you *are*.

When those moments come, treasure them. Gradually they'll come more often, and eventually freedom will be your default setting, your resting place, your home ground of being. You only need to have the willingness to be liberated, to be transformed and healed, and to surrender to what's being offered in this moment, and in every moment.

So find out how to give yourself fully. In giving yourself fully, you receive fully. When finally you let go of all that you're holding on to, *everything* is given to you in return.

As we deepen in this process, gradually relinquishing more and more control, we begin to really live from our heart. We listen from the heart, feel from the heart, and even think from the heart. And then we feel ourselves, and each other—profoundly, in all the richness of our shared being.

19.

Just Listening

Often when I'm working with people or groups, I'll offer instructions similar to those I just described to help people explore and allow the movement of whatever is happening in their experience. That movement can be intense! Emotional, physical, or energetic shifts can happen.

Perhaps because of my background as a musician, one of the most common ways I speak about this allowing is to describe it as *listening*.

Just listening is listening that is free of thinking. It is without an interpreter, or analyzer, or someone who compares. It is simply *allowing* listening. In the previous chapter I suggested a practice of literally listening in an auditory sense, but often I use the term more metaphorically. I invite people to "listen" to their bodies, for instance, or to their energy, or to their internal guidance system.

When I lead retreats, the schedule I have people follow includes a lot of unstructured or minimally structured time. It's important for people to have the opportunity to really drop in deeply and *listen*. But this instruction isn't only for retreats or formal practice sessions. This kind of listening is important all the time: listening to whether you're eating too much, for instance, or whether you're walking too quickly, or talking too quickly. Listening to where you're at emotionally. Listening to where others are at, and to what they need.

A good way to cultivate this listening is to stop from time to time and ask yourself:

What do I need right now?

Sometimes the answer will be obvious, but other times this or a similar question may reveal something under the surface, some unfelt need or impulse you haven't seen or acknowledged. Sometimes the answer may be, "Wow, I really don't know what I need," and that too is important to acknowledge, express, and feel. Whatever answer you get, whatever your condition is in any moment, it's important to be honest with yourself about where you actually are and how that is for you.

"How that is for you" may not match up with what you expect, what you want, or what you hope for, and so sometimes what's also present is disappointment or frustration. Recognizing and acknowledging what's *actually happening*, including that frustration or disappointment, will allow the energy of those feelings to move, rather than remaining stuck and gumming up your system.

On the other hand, sometimes when you check in with yourself, you'll find that things are actually better than you thought they were. Our habitual ways of thinking and processing our experience can sometimes blind us to how things are shifting for the better.

So cultivate living in a space of open receptivity. Sitting practice can of course be very helpful for this. Sitting silently in an amplified field of presence and awareness can facilitate a deepening and a strengthening of your energy body, which very much supports this kind of ongoing attention. There's a reason people have been doing these practices for a few thousand years. If they're approached with the right attitude, they work!

So what *is* the right attitude? It's the willingness to be available, to be vulnerable, to *not know*. And to be compassionate and gentle with yourself. To allow yourself to just be with *what is*, and to give yourself whatever comfort that you might need at any moment— patience, forgiveness, permission. A very innocent, open, and available state of mind, body, and heart.

A big part of the right attitude is also the willingness to be wrong! Being wrong can be delightful and is actually one of my favorite things to experience. Sometimes circumstances will quite suddenly reveal that something you were very certain about is not true at all. Although sometimes jarring or destabilizing, this can be an incredible blessing and an opportunity for great liberation if you can really take it in.

On the spiritual path, the way this most commonly shows up is around our expectations. People have so many expectations about how the spiritual path is going to unfold for them. Spiritual litera-ture is full of maps and models of spiritual progress, with steps and stages and sequences in which certain things unfold, and of course there are also the many personal stories of sages and teachers and the ways the process manifested for them. This is not a bad thing—these models and stories can be deeply inspirational and very impor-tant to many people's development.

Ultimately, though, preconceived ideas about what's going to happen will get in the way of perceiving reality directly. Without even consciously realizing it, you may define your experience in terms of those ideas. In that defining of experience, you've *identified* the experience, and in doing so you've added another layer to your own identity, a belief about where you're going and what will happen.

But reality doesn't always conform to our beliefs. Your expecta-tions about where this process will take you and what will happen along the way, and even your ideas about what awakening or spiritu-ality are, will be continually dismantled. At times this may be jarring, or shocking, or even disappointing, but gradually you'll dis-cover a certain joy in it. You'll find yourself surprised and delighted when the way you thought things were going to be turns out to be very different from how they actually are. Rather than being a nega-tive thing, this is instead a welcome discovery and an opportunity for the mind to relax and become more flexible.

◇◇◇◇

The way to unbelievable happiness is to relinquish your invest-ment in any position, in any belief system or identity, any set of expectations. It's not about being right or wrong at all, but about being willing to question your assumptions and see what's in front of you. It's about being open and available to what's *actually happening* and allowing *that* to show you the way.

Of course you won't always feel open and available. Sometimes you might feel closed, protected, or angry; irritated, tired, restless; or even just bored. If that's what's happening for you, then again, ask yourself, "What do I need?" Ask the question, and then relax, let go, and *just listen* to what's being communicated, even if it's something you don't want to hear. Often we try to push away what we don't want to feel, but our feelings are there to get our attention. Our feelings are asking us to listen.

My dad used to tell me, "You can't listen with your mouth open." Similarly, you also can't listen when you're busy telling yourself what you're hearing. If you're constantly telling yourself a story about what's happening, you're not really *experiencing* what's happening. This is why, again, allowing *not knowing* is key. It's not about cultivating ignorance or avoiding knowing; it's about letting go of *being the knower.*

Letting go of *knowing* is deeply healing. It softens your attention. It softens your body. It relaxes your nervous system, cultivating openness and peace in your physical form. It's lovely! It's pleasurable. So be sure to let that pleasure in. Let it permeate you. Let it nourish every cell in your body. And when it goes, let it go, and deeply allow whatever comes next.

20.

The Quality of Awareness

It's not just *that* you bring awareness to what's happening; it's *how* you bring awareness that makes all the difference. You can bring awareness to your experience in a way that causes you to be more identified, more held in, more contracted. But you can also bring awareness in a way that facilitates unwinding, and letting go, and the dissolving of the limited personal self.

How we think can enslave us, but it can also liberate us. This is the value of inquiry. What is inquiry, really? It's a different kind of questioning—questioning our thoughts, our impressions, our beliefs. You can question in such a way that you become more tightly wound up in thinking, more separate from reality, or you can question in a way that *dissolves the questioner*. When you begin truly to understand how that works, how to question and direct your awareness in such a way that the mind dissolves, then in a flash you're fully *right here*. Now there's no more "you" at all. There's just awareness.

Another way to think about it: Think of your mind as a projector, projecting its contents over the top of reality. What if you could go inside yourself and find the off-switch to that projector? When you turn off the projector, what's left is just awareness. And as long as we're speaking metaphorically, you could also approach it the other way around—turn *on* the awareness and outshine the projections. Whatever works for you. The point is that when you're not projecting, there's no "you" getting in the way, no identity.

Of course it's fine to have an identity; the personal self has its place and is obviously very useful in many contexts. But happiness means being free, right now, from whatever is burdening you, and for most people that is largely their identity. We all have our stuff: physical, emotional, psychological, circumstantial. But you can wake up; you can turn on awareness and turn off the projector, right now.

That's what *being here* is about: being here! When you're fully here, your heart will release its troubles. What emerges first may be tears, or fear, or even anger, depending on what you're burdened with. Once that's passed, though, you'll begin to sense this closeness, this nearness, this intimacy with everything. So if you're feeling uncomfortable, find out how to bring awareness to that discomfort. Now you're not pushing it away, or judging it, or comparing it to some other experience, but rather welcoming it with tenderness, patience, and compassion, and if needed, forgiveness, and even gratitude. Welcome this moment, however it appears.

When we're projecting, we're pushing, forcing our agenda onto reality. It's kind of aggressive, actually, but the truth is it's well-intended. It's a protective mechanism: our human body and mind doing their best to keep us safe. So no blame, no shame, no judgment. Instinct is just instinct, a reflex. So forgive your reflexes, every one. Even if they seem dark, or wrong, or bad, or inappropriate.

Eventually we begin to see the projector as the teacher. We realize, "I've been thinking that's them, but it's only the filter I'm looking through. Wow!" As soon as you see that clearly, opening starts to happen, awareness expands, and then every moment is a teaching; every person is a teacher. The teacher isn't just some guy writing a book, or speaking in front of a room. Of course that kind of teaching can be helpful, can point you in the right direction initially, but ultimately the teaching is right where you are, always.

◇◇◇◇

The mind can be fun, so enjoy it! As part of an awakened, integrated self, the mind can be a beautiful, miraculous manifestation of the universal field—just like everything else. How you think, how

THE UNBELIEVABLE HAPPINESS OF WHAT IS

you speak, and how you listen, all can be liberating. If you learn to play an instrument, you can make music. The mind is a kind of instrument, as is the body, and even the heart. So learn to play your human instrument, and you'll find that you're walking around in a miracle of discovery.

Even though you may not know how yet, gradually you'll begin to trust that the wisdom of life is literally what you are, what made you. So how could you *not* be able to access it? How could it *not* be available, right now, to you or anybody? That understanding opens the door to trusting, to allowing yourself to tune in to your experience, to becoming available for what's happening right now, so you're no longer fighting it, or resisting it, or trying to fix it, change it, understand it, or get rid of it.

Embrace and allow this moment so something much deeper can rise to the surface. This awakened, infinite intelligence that you are—that we *all* are—when *that* comes to the foreground, just surrender to it, and fully relax in complete, effortless stillness, exquisite balance. Then life is brand new, right here, right now. You can savor the flavors, smell the fragrance, hear the birds! And be free. And be happy.

21.

Transmission of the Flame

Even though you're reading a collection of words right now, the essential communication here is nonverbal. The true teaching is in the silence beneath the words—in the space within which these words arise.

The truth can't really be believed in, or even explained; it can only be experienced. You may read a spiritual book, or listen to a podcast, or come to see a teacher like me in person, and in that interaction find that there is a *direct experience* of the truth that, once glimpsed for the first time, can serve as your guide on the path. You only need to find out how to recognize that experience as it happens and give *that* your attention.

As I've said, there are no "teachers," not really, but there are people who can be helpful, hopefully, in offering a certain description of how to recognize your *own* inherent guidance system. When you're with someone—whether in person or by reading a book like this one—whose own perspective is free and unidentified, you may experience a kind of resonance. That resonance can facilitate a deep remembrance of who you truly are, and that remembrance is the entryway to your own guidance system. Traditionally this process is called *transmission*.

The experience of transmission can open you and expand you. It can activate all kinds of healing in your body and mind, physically and emotionally. Fundamentally what's happening is that pure awareness—that which you *truly are*—is coming into the foreground.

When you hear the word "transmission," you may think of a transmitter sending out some kind of signal. This implies that there's also a receiver—if there's a transmission, there must also be some kind of reception, right? Something must be "transmitted" from point A to point B. Spiritual transmission can sometimes be experienced that way—you connect with a powerful teacher or teaching, and all of a sudden you seem to get a kind of energy hit. You feel some power, some energy, that you seem to be receiving from that person.

But that's not what spiritual transmission truly is in its essence. As you become more familiar with your *own* deep openness, then that awakened consciousness in you becomes *enlivened* by the inter-action with a person who is resonating on the vibratory level of freedom. That *enlivening* brings the spacious presence of being that is *already yours* to the forefront of your experience—where you can no longer avoid it! Although it may feel like something is being given to you by that other person, in truth, transmission is a simultaneous giving and receiving of *yourself*.

Another way to describe it is to say that your *own* deep aware-ness has a certain resonant field. When you come into contact with a teacher who is operating from a place of openness, of freedom, you may find that the communication from that person resonates within you at a frequency that you normally wouldn't experience or notice. There's an attunement that happens, a kind of pull toward open-ness. Rather than being so focused in thought, you begin to slow down and notice sensations. You find yourself sensing into the breath, becoming more aware on an energetic level, fully engaged in the vibrancy of the present moment.

But even though it may seem initially like this is happening *because* of that other person, that some kind of energy is coming from outside of you, the truth is *that which you already are* is simply being awakened and enlivened by that which everything is—which is actually that very same awareness. When you really *tune in* to the field of transmission, your personal self dissolves, and you see that there's just this field of energy. It isn't flowing from point A to point B, from the so-called teacher to the so-called student—rather, it's flowing in all directions simultaneously.

That's what teaching really is. The stories you may have heard in which a student is acknowledged by the teacher—"That's it! You have it!"—refer to this transmission of the truth, this deep knowing. It's not an intellectual knowledge, but a deep, profound, felt recognition of being. It's falling in love on the highest level, where there's no attachment and no need. It's not personal—there is no person in it. There is no identity in it. It's a unified oneness.

The student feels the energetic flow or connection with the teacher and calls that transmission. But as the student wakes up, student and teacher mutually recognize each other *as* that energy, that source, that *being*. When that connection is happening, it can feel like you're in love. I felt that with my teachers. Profound gratitude and deep appreciation arise spontaneously with the recognition of our unified field, and it's always mutual. It doesn't go only one way. It *can't* go only one way.

◇◇◇◇

As the old saying goes, when your nose is clean, you can smell the flower. When you are open, openness is there for you. When you recognize your true nature, it recognizes you too. When you love the truth, the truth loves you. It's a mutual love affair. That's why someone who has a powerful glimpse of awakening will often drop everything to devote their entire life to it. They've seen directly that there's nothing more important than *that*. Everything else is ultimately transient, impermanent, empty.

If there's any real work to be done, it's allowing remnants of the personal self to be consumed in the fire of the transmission and transformed into light. The process is like alchemy, a kind of transmutation. *Whatever* you bring to this process, whatever's coming up in you as the transmission cooks your being, you naturally offer it into the space of awareness—whether it's emotion, physical issues, thoughts or beliefs about how things are, conclusions that you now see were not useful, or ideas about yourself that you now realize were limiting and not really true.

At some point you recognize that you *are* this awareness. You are this; we are this; everything is this. From that perspective there is no "we." There is no separation. Of course on a practical, ordinary level, we are separate individuals. There's you, and there's me. That's relative reality. But transmission is of the realm of the absolute. Although it can be imperfectly described, it can't really be understood intellectually.

Fortunately, you don't have to worry about understanding it intellectually. If you have the courage and you're ready, then you dive in and face whatever needs to be faced, whatever you were unwilling or just too unconscious to face before. The experience of transmission is an opportunity to completely surrender—not to some teacher, or teaching, or set of beliefs, but to the simple relief of finally letting go of all of that.

So surrender to that freedom. Surrender to the space that is beyond struggling, beyond all our conditioned, unsatisfactory circumstances. When you tune in to the transmission, to this radiant field of presence, then you are, at least for a while, free of all limited conditions. Freedom truly is the saving grace.

22.

Mirror of Truth

Encountering the mirror of transmission is an important step on the path for most of us, a vital pointing out of what the path actually is. Many people have awakening experiences without knowing what's happened to them. They realize something has changed, but they don't know what or why. They're not getting the feedback, or mirroring, that would help them understand what has happened. So that's what I'm offering here—a mirroring of that truth, and support for all the healing, breakdown, catharsis, and everything else that can happen along the way.

If you're familiar with traditional non-dual teachings, you may have heard that you should just forget all of that personal stuff—that "You are not the body, you are not the mind," and so on, and that your personal history, emotions, traumas, and conditioning are therefore beside the point. From the absolute perspective, that's true; awareness in and of itself is already complete, already perfect as it is. And yet, a blocked, unhealthy human system can be a real impediment on the spiritual path, making it much more difficult for you to recognize that perfect awareness. So there is actually great value in addressing your human-level issues and conditioning.

This aspect of the work can be challenging. Your human form is where you've lived for your entire life. It's the storehouse of your experience, both positive and negative. When you begin to open energetically, releasing long-held tensions in your body and mind, you may directly encounter the reasons those tensions exist in the first place. Old traumas that have been deeply buried in the nervous system can percolate up to the surface quite suddenly. You need to take care of yourself and continually do the necessary clearing work as this happens.

People are often surprised that even after decades of spiritual practice, unhealthy aspects of the personality that have still gone unseen can erupt unexpectedly into the light. As uncomfortable as this can be, it's actually a good thing. The more you can allow that material to emerge, the greater the opportunity for healing. Taking care of your body, and just being gentle with yourself, can help you relax and allow that emergence so that deep healing can happen.

This process can be painful, but gradually you learn to just go with it—to flow with the breakthroughs, the breakdowns, the disorientations, the re-groundings. There's a kind of ecology of flow that you begin to tune in to, that you begin to trust. Gradually you accept that this life is not your own. You don't own this life. You're not in control of this life. So you learn to allow yourself to be guided—you give yourself to awareness and let what needs to happen, happen. Awakening is a flow that will unfold your life like a rose, and as it takes you, you'll find yourself living in a constant state of discovery.

◇◇◇◇

Spiritual transmission is always here, always available. If a student is open and available, transmission can't *not* be given. When you are open to it, you find you are filled with it. As I've said, in that moment, it can feel like you're receiving something from outside you, but in truth you're only learning to directly perceive that which you've always had and always been.

The experience of transmission can be pleasant, even blissful at times, but it can also be intense or agitating. You may reach a point where suddenly you want to shut it off and run out the door. Our conditioning is to seek comfort and resist discomfort, so when this happens, we assume something's not right, that there's a problem, or that we're doing something wrong. In actuality, though, that kind of discomfort is actually a good indication that the process is working.

I often speak of transmission as a kind of cooking process, and sometimes you need to cook for an extended period of time. This is part of the value of retreats. If you've been on a silent retreat, you know it's not necessarily a uniformly pleasant experience. You might feel fabulous at times, but at some point things will inevitably get pretty challenging. Again, this process often precipitates the emergence of material we've ignored or repressed, and that can be difficult, but even the simple experience of your body relaxing slightly more than it's used to can produce some fear or anxiety. As you relax, you *feel more deeply*, and that can be a little intense.

So there is a kind of physical reality to the transmission in that sense, where your experience is amplified, intensified in the space of presence. When I was with my various teachers, I learned to make use of that experience by completely surrendering into that presence. The words they were saying, although sometimes deeply inspiring, were ultimately less important. The transmission was in the silence beneath those words, and that was the true teaching.

Even to call it "teaching" may still be a little misleading. What you eventually realize very directly is that there is no teaching. There is only the profound intimacy of giving and receiving ourselves simultaneously in the simple reality of *what is*.

◇◇◇◇

I remember being part of a group of older students of one of my teachers. After each week's meeting, we'd be hanging around together and would all do a kind of assessment: On a scale of one to ten, how powerful was the transmission that night? It seems funny in retrospect, but that was our perspective at the time. Eventually I began to realize that this was a misunderstanding on our part of what was actually happening. Many of us were looking to repeat experiences we'd had in the past—dramatic openings, spiritual highs, and so on. Those experiences seemed to indicate progress (and were also very enjoyable!), and so we measured our new experiences based on the past, on our ideas about what should be happening.

But the past is never a reliable guide to the future, especially when it comes to this kind of work. As you deepen in awareness, you integrate that deepening, and now it's your baseline, your new default setting. People often try to go back and reproduce dramatic spiritual experiences they've had, and then wonder why they're not having the same big blowouts again. But the truth is, having the "same" experience may no longer seem like a blowout at all because now you've been living in that space—living *as* that space.

So stop and notice if you're allowing yourself to live as that space, right now. Notice if you're open to the transmission of this moment, right now. Or notice if you're resisting something or your mind is wandering off somewhere. If it is, gently bring yourself back, and notice what you're sensing, what's going on in your body. Are you relaxed, or is there tension? As always, drop in and feel the natural movement of the breath, letting it breathe by itself, and if you're able to, just relax as that open, spacious awareness that perceives *whatever* is happening right now.

◇◇◇◇

There is nothing to follow outside of yourself. Ultimately there is no teacher, or teaching, or path. There is only this simple truth of *being* that is what you fundamentally are. As this truth becomes more foreground for you, you'll find that life really is all about learning, not just intellectually (although that happens too), but in a much broader sense—learning to allow yourself to be guided. You are guided in each moment. You only need to learn to recognize that guidance and let yourself follow it.

23.

Beyond Understanding

We naturally want to grasp things intellectually. We want to feel secure in our understanding. We want to feel like we're on the right track, and that we're not wasting our time, not just spinning our wheels. But transformation is a mystery. It is fundamentally not graspable on an intellectual level. Our attempts to grasp it or understand it actually interfere with it.

So take the opportunity awareness offers you and relinquish the struggle of *trying to understand*. Step out of the past and out of the future. Stop worrying about where you came from and where you're going. Allow yourself to really settle and ground, right here in this moment. Let your heart open. Let your being expand. Now your body can heal, your mind can unwind. Give yourself some space and some time to *just be here* and let transformation happen by itself.

People often ask, "Well, what is my role then? How can I participate in this process? If I'm not supposed to interfere with it, *how* do I not interfere with it?"

The answer is by noticing where you *are* interfering with it. Take a step back and, with gentle attention, observe your habitual patterns of defensiveness and resistance, and in particular the ways you repress your emotional energies. As you bring awareness to these dynamics, you'll find they begin to shift and unwind. What's been held in begins to release, and those patterns begin to dissolve in the space that awareness creates.

I want to emphasize again that nobody—nobody!—really knows what's going on. From a conventional perspective, this might sound alarming, but as that understanding really sinks in, I think you'll find it's actually a great relief. In the awakening process, we move from the profound insecurity of being a human organism that wants to survive and be comfortable to the profound security of *being awareness itself*. We move from the instability of needing to be grounded to an openness of being that is inherently groundless.

Of course even talking about moving from one place to another is a bit misleading. We don't have to go anywhere to find awareness. In fact, we can't find it! Rather, we are found by it. It reveals itself to us. What we can do is notice where we're in the way of our own discovery process. That's the essence of all spiritual practice—seeing clearly where we are holding on and preventing ourselves from moving. We assume we can take some action to get ourselves out of the way. We think we can "get" enlightened, but that's a misunderstanding. We can't get what we already are! All we can do is bring compassionate attention to what's in the way. The rest takes care of itself.

All you need is the mirror of this moment. Can you look into that mirror and not recoil from what you see, what you feel, or what you think? Can you simply listen, see, and feel, free of judgments and conclusions—even as judgments and conclusions continue to arise? Rest as awareness, even as your reactions and judgments continue to arise in the space that awareness creates.

The judging mind is part of being human. So forgive yourself for being human; in fact, be thankful for it. Forgiveness and gratitude are great healers of the mind and the heart, and as human beings we need that healing. We've all taken a lot of damage in this life. We have to allow ourselves to be healed.

So I want to thank you for being here, right now, and for your willingness to surrender your beliefs, your ideas of who you think you are, and what your life is about. Thank you for being willing to *not know* what's happening; for being willing even to be vulnerable or afraid, or sad or angry, if that's what's arising; and for bringing ten-derness, gentleness, patience, and caring to whatever your nervous system is going through so you can continually return to *just being right here*.

So let yourself drop into the space of awareness. Allow this openness to be the foreground of your experience. Let your thoughts, your emotions, your body, and everything else simply rest in that space, allowing whatever movement needs to happen for them. Be aware of your habits of struggle, of trying to control your experience, but at the same time don't reject or repress those habits. Don't worry about trying to fix them or get rid of them. What frees us is not stop-ping the struggle, but rather our willingness to *allow* the struggle.

Allowing is the path, the doorway to this spacious awareness that you already are, and it's what lets the light come forward. These moments when we discover that light are what motivates us to con-tinue on this bumpy road to freedom. Even when we're at the bottom of our despair, the spirit continues to burn bright.

When in my own process I was finally able to relinquish the struggle to understand, it was extraordinarily freeing. I was free of being the knower, free to *not know*, and to just be relaxed, just be open. What a relief it was to let go of control! So I invite you to let go of control too. Feel how amazing it is to *just be*.

24.

Working with Belief

As I said way back in the introduction, our unexamined beliefs about life, about truth, and about ourselves are some of the biggest impediments on the spiritual path. Our beliefs are not separate from our identities—that is, *who we think we are*—and ironically, the spiritual identity is one of the most difficult of all to see through.

We create systems of belief in order to function, to navigate our human lives. But we come to a point on the spiritual path where all our beliefs must unwind. It isn't that we necessarily get rid of our beliefs; rather, we simply realize that our beliefs are not us. When people are suffering, they are 100 percent identified with their beliefs. They can't see any difference between their beliefs and themselves. A threat or challenge to their beliefs is experienced as a personal threat to themselves and triggers their survival instincts very directly.

But when you open spiritually, you move into the realm of *not knowing*, and in a sense you move *beyond belief*. Your beliefs don't need to be eliminated, or even intentionally changed. Again, they may have necessary and positive functions. Rather, by bringing your beliefs into conscious awareness, you move beyond them and into a direct experience of life that is no longer mediated by the *filter* of belief.

Now you have a completely fresh perspective, outside the realm of memory and your usual strategies for making meaning of your life. This can feel like an altered state of consciousness, especially at first. Everything is new, everything is fresh. You've gone beyond the known, beyond the expected. You're an explorer in unknown territory, endlessly surprised and delighted by the unexpected.

◇◇◇◇

In order to work with your beliefs, you first need to be able to identify them. One way to do this is to pay careful attention whenever you feel triggered or defensive in an interaction with another person. This is almost always a symptom of a belief being challenged, whether subtly or overtly. In any situation like that, anytime you catch yourself being triggered, you can bring that unexamined belief into consciousness by feeling deeply into your own discomfort and restlessness.

You can also do this by yourself. Tune in to your body, into your heart, right now. Notice in particular any discomfort or uneasiness or unsettledness in your body. Breathe into that discomfort. Feel into that uneasiness or unsettledness. As you enter into the depth of that feeling, ask yourself, "Why do I feel this way?" You'll probably find that your mind has an answer—a story about exactly why, where the feeling comes from, and what it means. That story is your belief about it.

This can of course get much more complicated when other people are involved, but here's a very simple, benign example. Say you find yourself in a situation where you're working with other people on a project of some kind and your collaborators are moving more slowly than you would like. In this situation you might feel restless, anxious, or frustrated. If you stop, take a few breaths and ask yourself why you're feeling those things. You might find yourself thinking, *These people are holding me back!* In this way you've identified a *belief* that you are being "held back" by these other people.

But is that belief true? Your collaborators are just doing what they're doing, and you're just having the reactions you're having. In fact, what you have in your field of awareness is just sensation—feeling, discomfort—and maybe a mental sense that you *don't want* that feeling or discomfort. The interpretation, "These people are holding me back" is secondary, a kind of contraction of energy around the actual lived experience of that interaction. Seeing that contraction for what it is can allow it to dissolve, leaving you with only the direct experience of the situation as it actually is, and allowing you to meet and engage it fully and consciously.

It helps to take a step back from your beliefs and see them for the energetic movements that they are. People instinctively believe their beliefs because those beliefs *feel* right, because they have a certain charge. When you discharge—when you open your energetic field and allow that energy to move—you're no longer caught in the energy of the belief. Now the story is suddenly much less convincing. Free of your interpretations and conclusions, you can meet the situation as it actually is, with flexibility and openness.

Moving beyond belief is a description of what happens when authentic attention permeates that which you're struggling with. It's not something you *do*, exactly, but rather a description of a change in perspective. When you enter into the essential feeling that underlies the story you're telling yourself about what you're experiencing, you are able to be truly honest with yourself about *how* you are struggling. Now your story about the struggle—your *belief* about it—dissolves, and you're left with what's actually happening in this moment.

The simplest way a belief is created is by defining or naming some aspect of your experience in relation to yourself. If you have fear, for instance, and you say "I'm afraid," you give your fear a name, an identity, and plant the seed of a belief. Initially, this is fine. It's how our minds work. We name and categorize the many things we experience, and this can obviously be very useful in many areas. But continually telling yourself "I'm afraid, I'm afraid," strengthens that belief, and strengthens your identity as the person who is afraid.

So instead, see if you can allow yourself to experience that same feeling or sensation without labeling it "fear" or telling yourself "I'm afraid." Now you are experiencing it *beyond* belief, outside of the realm of projection. Now you can experience it *directly*, without preconceptions, and you may be surprised to discover that it's not quite what you thought it was.

◇◇◇◇

If belief is arising, how do I engage it? How do I work with it in a way that's going to be productive?

The first thing is to become aware of your belief and to recognize that it's in the way. What's going on may not always be obvious in these cases. You may not have a simple thought, like *I believe this.* The roots of your belief may be hidden.

Your first indication that a belief is in the way is usually a reaction of some kind, often in the form of tension in the body. Someone contradicts something you've said, for instance, and you "stiffen," or tense up. It can also appear as an emotional reaction—something unexpected happens, and you get angry, or feel anxious or afraid.

So as this happens, look for the immediate source of your tension, or your emotional pain. Observe the feelings that come up—the sadness, the disappointment, the sense of unworthiness—and the stories that attach to them: "I'm not good enough." "Nobody wants me." "I'm not living up to my potential."

Beneath all these stories are what I would call your *core* beliefs, or the truth of your condition. Comprehending that truth—not as an idea or concept, but directly, viscerally—will transform you completely. When you speak, or even think that truth, it will resonate through your whole nervous system and open you up.

Now, do you have to go searching for your core beliefs? Not at all. You only need to be aware in your body, in your nervous system, and in your emotional body, your energy body. When the core belief emerges, you'll get very clear kinesthetic feedback. You will *feel* that it's true.

25.

If It Feels Good, Be It!

In the 1960s, we used to have a saying: If it feels good, do it! I think that could really use an update: If it feels good, *be it.*

We perceive reality through the senses. In each moment, seeing is happening. Hearing is happening. Feeling is happening. The senses are always happening. But often we're so caught up in the mind, in the thought-realm, that we barely experience our senses. They're in the background, obscured by our endless internal chatter. We allow our mental world to completely cut us off from the reality of sensing—of *sensuality.*

Although it's often left out of spiritual discussions, I want to emphasize that word: "sensuality." How often do we experience this moment as sensual? The word implies a kind of richness, perhaps a blissfulness. Do you experience ordinary moments as sensual? Or do you just observe them in some detached way?

Sensuality is a kind of deepening into sensation. It's an intimacy with sensing, a closeness that eventually dissolves the separate self. It's the bringing of a kind of heartfulness to our experience, rather than merely sensing in a detached way. It is a full welcoming of, and moving toward, *what is.*

Intimacy with *being* is deeply sensual. It's rich with feeling. When you begin dissolving into this presence, the energy gets thick, and experience becomes very rich on both sensory and feeling levels. The simplest sensations can be fascinating and profoundly pleasurable. You may look at another person and be overwhelmed with love, even though you may not know them personally at all. This deep sensitivity arises naturally from the growing insight that *there is nothing and no one outside of yourself.*

By default we interpret this world as a place outside ourselves that we, as discrete individuals, pass through. But when we drop into the space of *being*—when we *become* the space of being—then suddenly we see there is no outside, and there never was an outside. Now our perspective undergoes a radical shift. If there is nothing outside of us, then everything *is* us.

When you begin to realize that everything you perceive is *actually you yourself*, your relationship to your experience turns inside out. The quality of your attention shifts, and each moment is intensely sensual, intimate, immediate. You begin to relate to all that you encounter with love, with tenderness and compassion, and also with forgiveness for the parts of yourself that are acting out, that are causing harm, that are difficult to be around. This is not a mental sort of compassion, a result of some decision to be compassionate; rather, it's simply your natural response to the understanding that some parts of yourself are struggling.

So just being here, right now, is all you need to find your way: listening and sensing, without letting thought or interpretation get ahead of what's happening; feeling without resistance, without telling yourself a story about what the feeling means; or if resistance or internal storytelling is happening, then letting it happen, but gently detaching from it, allowing it to move into the background. Let yourself be a sensual sentient being. You'll find that life becomes completely fulfilling in even the most mundane, unremarkable kinds of moments.

So many people come to me and say, "I just want my heart to open up. I don't want to be in my head so much. I don't want to be so cut off." As human beings, we all want to find out how to connect, how to love, and really, how to be human. Awakening is the best way—in fact the only way—to become fully, authentically human.

From the awakened perspective, you no longer need to know what's happening. You don't need to understand what I'm talking about. You can just trust this moment, right now. When you're enjoying a moment, there's naturally openness. There's nothing blocking the pleasure of that moment. An amazing richness permeates everything.

When we have these glimpses of awakening, these moments of freedom, the richness and fullness of life are vividly present. This is what gives life meaning—this is what it is to be truly alive. When we're living primarily in a mental world, we're not really aligned with aliveness. We may barely notice the physical world we're passing through, or even our own feelings. We're alive, yes, but we're disconnected, disembodied.

But in these moments when we awaken, when we touch our truth, we fall deeply into alignment, deeply into embodiment. There's a deep gratitude for the richness of each moment, and the willingness to face what maybe you haven't been able to face up until now. Now we have the courage to do the real human work, the alchemy, transforming the dark side into the light—allowing the lead to become gold.

So right now, take a moment to allow yourself to open into this vast space of being. Take this opportunity to surrender into fullness, into just being aliveness. Allow your full sensuality to emerge: opening into ever-wider openness. Letting your body unwind. Letting your heart unwind. Letting your mind unwind.

◇◇◇◇

Awakening changes everything. It offers you a new approach to life, a new set of options. That's not to say all your old personal dynamics vanish—the personality has a lot of momentum! But even though you may still experience at least some of the same old automatic reactivity, you'll find yourself welcoming it rather than pushing it away. You'll see those reactions arising within the space of awareness. You'll see how they work, how they function. You'll see very, very clearly that your thoughts and reactions are no longer—and never actually were—who you are.

The amazing thing about this process is that the insights keep coming. The discoveries and awakenings and openings are ongoing. Awakening is not just a one-time thing! It goes on and on.

Always remember that your path is unique. The essence of it is universal—this awareness, this presence is common to everyone. But how this process unfolds for each individual is completely unique. So you have to find out what's working for you and how it is working for you. Take care not to get too caught up in anyone else's description of their own path or practice regimen.

That's not to say you don't seek out advice or that you don't try different practices; I'm obviously offering a lot of both in this book, and there's a lot of other good stuff out there that you can benefit from as well. But ultimately you've got to find out *right now*, in this and every moment, what's actually working for you. And it could change in the next moment! There's no universal formula. There's just the opportunity to open to each moment, trusting what's showing up and finding out how to surrender to it—how to say *yes*.

26.

Clearing, Grounding, Integrating, and Expanding: A Seven-Step Protocol

I want to offer now a series of exercises I've found to be very useful in helping people stabilize as they deepen in presence and insight. I call this series "A Seven-Step Protocol for Clearing, Grounding, Integrating, and Expanding."

People can of course access presence in ways that are profound and transformative without doing practices or techniques at all. But what I've observed over time is that although many people have spiritual openings or expansions, they often fail to integrate and then fully embody those experiences. They may initially become very open energetically and spiritually, but if their body and mind are not conditioned to handle that kind of energy, then that transformation can't really take root and fully stabilize.

A lot of the reason for this is the way energy can become stuck in the body. It's important from the beginning to *clear* that energy. As I've said already, you need to be a channel for energy rather than a receptacle. So it's important to work with your physical body, your emotions, and your thoughts in such a way as to facilitate the freeing up of that energy, so you can allow it to move through and out of you.

There can be other issues as well. If your energetic channels are blocked by unprocessed physical and emotional material, spiritual opening can be accompanied by destabilizing physical or emotional symptoms. Some people experience involuntary movements, for instance, or mood swings and emotional instability. So it's important to also do the work of training the body and working with your emotions. Spiritual transformation is a full-scale operation!

Additionally, people can be imbalanced in their development. Individuals can become very developed and sometimes even quite powerful spiritually, but often there remain challenging aspects of their human psychodynamic structure that haven't been fully examined. These difficult aspects of ourselves, as challenging as they can be, need to be brought fully into consciousness, healed, and integrated. This work facilitates that process of healing and integration.

I think it's important to continue with these or similar practices no matter how enlightened you get. Think of it as psychic hygiene. We're human beings, and we'll always have human experiences that need to be cleared out of our system. Our bodies need to release tension. Our hearts need to release emotion. It's important to embrace and allow these natural functions. As I've often said, spirituality is about fully embracing our humanity, not simply transcending it.

◇◇◇◇

The attitude with which you approach these or any practices is very important. This isn't about just applying a formula or performing a series of steps to produce a specific result. Rather, I invite you to approach this process with an open mind and a non-expectant heart, and with a spirit of openness and curiosity. Do these exercises not with some idea of what will happen, but simply to do them, without expecting anything at all. Let yourself be surprised! Be an explorer in unknown territory and a scientist in your own spiritual laboratory.

Don't worry about how much time you spend on each exercise, or whether you do them all, or even what order you do them in. I'm presenting these exercises in a particular order, but that's mainly for the sake of convenience. You can begin with the first one, but as you'll see, it will sometimes make more sense to begin with the last. Others can be done together or simultaneously. What's most important is that you stay tuned in to your own process and find what works for you personally.

So when should you do these exercises? When it's obvious that there's blocked energy—in other words, when repressed feeling or emotion isn't able to move or isn't even conscious—you need to clear that blockage and free that energy to move. This kind of blockage can manifest as nervous energy or tension in the body or as a kind of nonspecific feeling of fear or free-floating anxiety. Obsessive thinking can be a clue as well—often racing, repetitive thoughts hide unprocessed, uncleared emotions beneath the surface.

While doing any of these exercises, you might experience other types of energy release. You might spontaneously begin laughing, or crying. If you do, let it happen! Let your body release whatever it needs to release. Often people think they need to know *why* they're laughing or especially why they're crying. They think if they're crying, something must be wrong.

The truth, though, is that there isn't necessarily any specific content associated with this kind of emotional release. Emotions, as I've often said, are just a movement of energy. Our thoughts and beliefs about our feelings—where they come from, what they mean, what "causes" them—usually just get in the way of that natural movement.

◇◇◇◇

When doing any kind of practice, it's important to stay focused on what's *actually happening* right now. It's easy to become future-focused—to *try* to accomplish something or cause some change to happen. If you find yourself beginning these exercises with the intention of getting something done or forcing some change to happen, then stop and take a step back. Relax for a few moments, and see if you can let go of your ideas about what you're doing and what it's going to do for you. Let all that go, then gently begin again.

After each exercise, take a moment to stop and notice where you're at. Notice how you're feeling, how energy is flowing, how your mental state has shifted. After clearing, it's important to give yourself some space to ground, which then allows integration and expansion to follow. So take that time, give yourself that space. There's no rush! There's only this moment.

STEP 1: THE SIMPLE BREATH

Whenever I'm working with someone and I become aware that they need to clear energy, the first thing I have them do is take a *simple breath.*

Begin with the open, grounded posture I recommended earlier in the book when discussing meditation. Sit in a chair, either leaning back or sitting upright, whichever is comfortable for you. If you sit upright, take care to sit so that you're balanced and relaxed rather than holding yourself in a rigid posture of some kind. You might sit so that your hips are slightly higher than your knees to avoid tension in the hips. Place your feet flat on the ground, and rest your palms facing downward on your thighs. Loosen your waistband if you need to so you can breathe comfortably from your belly.

Now relax. Let your jaw naturally drop open, so you're not stretching your mouth or creating more tension, but just letting the mouth be open. Inhale deeply through your open mouth, letting the belly fill with air and then letting the chest fill with air. Then release the breath and exhale, again through the open mouth, letting the chest and belly fall.

Inhale deeply, then release—and relax! You don't need to exert a lot of energy or intention toward sucking in the breath. You don't need to hold your breath at the top of the inhale. And you don't need to forcefully push the air out again. In the gentlest possible way, simply breathe in and let your lungs fill completely; then, just as gently, let the air flow back out again.

Try this a few times in a row—not too many, maybe three or so—and then sit and breathe normally, and pay attention to the sensations in your body. Notice also if there's any shift in your mental activity, your state of mind, or your emotions or feelings. You may find you feel more relaxed, physically looser.

If you were feeling stressed, you may find those feelings are a bit more diffuse now. That's why I start with the simple breath. It's really the most basic and I think the most well-used breath, and the best way to begin any kind of clearing.

STEP 2: THE BREATH WITH A SIGH

Sighing is a natural mechanism, a release of physical and emotional tension that humans perform quite instinctively. People have conditioned themselves unknowingly to hold in tension, to hold in stress, and most of the time they don't even know they're doing it. Sighing is a release of tension. It's getting a load off your shoulders. It's letting go.

Once again, sit comfortably, and take a deep, relaxed breath, just as you did in the previous step. As the breath flows back out again, let yourself make a simple, relaxed, familiar sound: *aaaaahhhhh*. As you breathe in again, you might even lift your shoulders a little bit, and then let them fall and relax, as again you breathe out a deep sigh of relief: *aaaaahhhhh*.

As with the first exercise, do a few of these, and then sit quietly for a bit and tune in to your body, into your feelings. Feel the breath in the belly, and notice any sensations that may be arising. How are you feeling? Has anything shifted?

By beginning to bring in sound as well as breath, you bring in both energy and expression. As you breathe in, you energize your body, and the sound of the sigh resonates through your tissues and helps that energy circulate, enlivening your lungs, your heart, and your whole energy system. And of course sound is expressive, and a sigh is a release of emotion, a relaxing into what you're actually feeling in this moment.

Through our conditioning we've learned to hold back feeling, to restrict ourselves emotionally, and so those energies become blocked in our nervous system. Our bodies can feel a bit like hard, dry soil that's never been properly cultivated, but as you learn to breathe freely, consciously, you begin to cultivate the tissues of your body. You vibrate them, energize them, and gradually your body comes back to life. You regain energy and vitality.

The reason the breath has been a focus of practice in so many spiritual traditions is that it is fundamentally energy. The breath is the vehicle for what in Eastern traditions is often called *qi* or *prana*. Many of us have become energetically depleted, so by bringing awareness to the breath, we can begin to bring more energy back into our system.

STEP 3: TONING

The third step also involves both breath and sound. We are expressive beings, and what's often missing in traditional spirituality is an outlet for that expression. We need to move sound through our body to express ourselves.

Many people hold themselves back and rarely or never fully express in this way. This holding back creates energy blockages, particularly in the throat, but often also in the heart and lung areas. The practice of toning—of using the voice to produce long-held tones—vibrates and enlivens these areas, helping to loosen those blockages and release that energy to flow freely through the body.

Once again, sit, relax, and inhale deeply. This time, as you exhale, use your voice. With your mouth open and your jaw relaxed, let out a very long tone: *AAAAAAAAAHHHHH.*

Let the sound continue until the end of the exhale, but don't force it; let it come to an end naturally. Now try another. This time, try a different sound: *OOOOOOOOHHHHH.* As with the other exercises, do this a few more times, using whichever of the two sounds feels better to you, and then stop, relax, and take a few minutes to feel into your body, into your breath, into your senses.

Try this in whatever way you like—louder or softer, more or less forcefully. Notice what happens. How does your body feel? How does your heart feel?

STEP 4: YAWNING

Often when you start doing these breath practices, you'll quite naturally find yourself yawning—and that's good! Yawning is a great way of moving energy, a natural mechanism by which the body replenishes and reenergizes itself.

So this next exercise is, simply, to yawn. You may have already found yourself yawning naturally while doing the previous exercises. If so, great! If you haven't, then try a sort of pseudo-yawn now. Open your mouth and breathe in just as if you were yawning and you'll probably find yourself yawning for real very shortly. And then, once again, stop, relax, and check in with yourself, with your body, with your feelings.

Yawning moves energy—that's why we do it! Like sighing, it's a natural release of tension. So you're facilitating a kind of natural functioning of your energy system, which has often been conditioned not to allow energy to move. When the movement of energy is blocked, you aren't able to integrate change and growth, because you have no space for them. In order to grow, you need to be a clear channel through which energy can move. You need your mind open and your body open so you can allow transformation to take you.

STEP 5: TAPPING THE CHEST

This next exercise can be done by itself, or along with any of the others.

Hold your hands in front of you, palms facing upward. Put your fingers together and curl them inward slightly, so each hand forms a U shape. Now bring your hands to your chest, and with your curled fingers, tap repeatedly along your upper chest area, just below the collarbone. Gently and continuously tap along the whole upper chest area, from the sternum all the way out to the ends of the collarbone near the shoulder joints, then back again. Notice the sound and vibration resonating in your chest, and observe how it energizes and enlivens your bodily structure.

You can also combine this exercise with the others. Try tapping while doing the simple breath, or the sigh, or the toning, and of course at any time you may find yourself yawning. Again, don't feel bound by the sequence in which I've presented these exercises. As I said at the beginning, the "right" order in which to do them is the order that, through experimentation, you find works for you.

STEP 6: EYE EXERCISES

In the late 1970s I was a student of Anna Kaye, a well-known author and practitioner of the Bates method, a series of eye exercises intended to help strengthen the vision, improve visual acuity, and so forth. Over the years I've found that some of these exercises help release energy in much the same way we've been doing with the breath. You may have encountered similar eye exercises in yoga, classical hypnosis, or therapeutic modalities like EMDR (eye movement desensitization and reprocessing) and hypnotherapy.

Begin again with quiet sitting and the simple breath; then close your eyes and take a few moments to tune in to your body. Once you've settled in, open your eyes.

Now move your eyes horizontally all the way over to the left, then all the way over to the right, and then back to the left again. Continue moving your eyes back and forth, gently and without strain, at whatever speed is comfortable for you. After doing this three or four times, close your eyes. Take a deep breath, then let it out again. Relax and tune in, and notice if there's been any change in your state or how you're feeling.

Try different variations of this exercise. You can move your eyes at different speeds or back and forth different numbers of times. You can also move your eyes diagonally—back and forth from upper left to lower right or from upper right to lower left.

Our eyes are deeply connected to the way our minds process information and memory. As a result, these exercises are powerful and could stir up some feelings or bring up unexpected memories. If this happens, stop and bring yourself back to this moment with the simple breath. Breathe in, then out. Follow it with a sigh, if it feels right. Then rest your attention in the breath, rising and falling in your belly, and as best you can, allow those feelings and sensations to move through you, and let yourself ground.

STEP 7: EXPRESSING THE TRUTH OF THE CONDITION

Emotion is the natural weather system of the human body, and yet so often we hold it back, we repress that natural movement. We may also invest our emotions with meaning, developing beliefs that support our holding them back. It's important to learn to free our emotions and allow them to move as they will, to release that energy and allow it to recirculate. One of the most important ways to do this is verbal expression.

What I often refer to as the "condition" is simply where you're at and what's happening. When you *express the truth of the condition*, you expose the essence, the essential core of the feeling that's being experienced, and by exposing it, you free it to move.

So sit quietly, and after allowing yourself to settle, speak into the space of awareness. Express as clearly as possible exactly what you're feeling. It could be a personal frustration, or a longing, or an unanswered question. Speak your truth, whatever it is in this moment, into the space of listening. Let it resonate through the space, and through your body. How does that feel? How do *you* feel?

Now take a deep breath, let yourself relax, and express that truth again. You may now find that you slightly change how you're expressing it—the tone, the wording, even the content may shift— and that's fine. Simply notice how it shifts. *Feel* how it shifts.

Express your truth as many times and in as many ways as you need to: "I want something." "I don't want something." "I need guidance." "I'm lonely." "I'm afraid." Whatever your truth is, the expression of it will activate and free the energy that is caught up in holding it. Once that energy begins to move, then breathe, release, and allow that movement to happen.

This is different from telling yourself (or someone else) the *story* or narrative of your situation or condition. The narratives we create to explain our experience to ourselves can become defenses, ways we prevent energy from moving. But if you are able to truly express where you're at from a place of honesty and openness, then immediately the held-in energy of the story will begin to move again. Expression can discharge the energy of the emotion, just as the eye and breath exercises can. These are all ways of discharging and recirculating the natural, flowing energy of your body, mind, and heart.

Even if your truth is as simple as just wanting something to happen, express that wanting. Breathe into that wanting and allow it to reveal itself for what it is. It may be wanting to be free of some discomfort or anxiety. It may be the core wanting that drives the spiritual search. Whatever it is, allowing it to come fully into consciousness and to be seen and heard for what it is will be deeply healing and freeing.

If you find yourself in a space of expectation—of demanding results—then *begin* with step 7. Before doing anything else, express the truth of what it is you actually want, right now. "I want to get rid of this pain." "I want to clear this emotion." "I'm tired of being angry." "I'm tired of being afraid." Really acknowledging what's true—starting right where you're at—will often get things moving right away. Then you can move on to the simple breath, or whichever of these practices is right for you in this moment.

27.

Offering into Awareness

I want to expand a bit on step 7, the exercise I described in the previous chapter as "expressing the truth of the condition." Often the best thing you can do in the face of reality is to listen, allow yourself to feel deeply, and then express the truth of what you're experiencing— and thereby *offer* it into the space of awareness.

If you can simply describe what's happening for you right now— with no particular agenda and drawing no conclusions—that expression can carry you into the transformational learning process that is freedom itself. What you're describing may be challenges, problems, or difficulties you're having, but you're not looking for answers or solutions. This isn't problem-solving time; rather, it's problem-dissolving time. Your expression is an *offering into awareness*. In offering up your struggle, you release it, and what you'll find is that in that offering, awareness releases you also.

Again, this is more than just telling your story or recounting a narrative about your suffering. It can begin that way, but what eventually emerges is the expression of the *truth* of the emotion beneath your struggle. Now that previously held-in emotion can finally begin to move. Initially this movement can feel threatening to the ego, and may be uncomfortable or even alarming at first. But as you learn to relax and allow that movement, you realize it's no longer about the meaning of the emotion, but rather about the raw energy of it. Now that emotion is no longer threatening—it's just energy, just movement. Your body can relax and stop holding back the grief, the fear, the anxiety, the anger. That which you've been repressing can emerge, move, and be cleared from your system.

As you learn to allow expression to arise from the space of deep listening, you'll find that listening includes your body, your mind, and your heart, and that it also goes way, way beyond any of those. Whether or not you know or experience it consciously, you are inherently intimate with the vastness from which that listening arises.

As I've said over and over again, it's okay to be human. It's okay to have whatever struggle, whatever condition is arising right now. If you don't think it's okay, ask yourself: *"Why* is it not okay?" After all, it is what's happening. So why would you deny it? What does that get you, to deny your humanity or the conditions that are being given to you right now, however difficult or challenging they might be?

Let yourself be the space of awareness. Rest in this vast space of deep listening. Give yourself permission to relinquish all struggle, all resistance, all control. There's no need to accomplish anything. Freedom has already accomplished itself.

◇◇◇◇

I experience a lot of grief and frustration when I look out at the world and seem to see nothing but injustice, inequity, and unconsciousness. It seems very righteous to feel that grief, but at the same time I'm so frustrated and I feel powerless to do anything.

So there's a *feeling* of helplessness and hopelessness. A feeling of not being able to take action. Try to really allow that feeling. Relax into that feeling. See if there's anything beneath the feeling, anything else wanting to be expressed.

If I'm honest, I feel like I'm failing to serve. I'm not giving enough, not serving enough. It's like I'm too selfish.

That's it! That's what you needed to offer up. The real truth of your pain was that: "I'm not serving enough; I'm too selfish." Now that you've expressed that pain, you can open, and your field can expand.

Very often that's all you need to do. Just *offer* your truth into the space of awareness. Simply expressing the truth of the condition you're struggling with can lift that burden from your heart. What will happen next—what changes you might make, what action you might take—can now arise naturally, and you get to have the awesome pleasure of seeing what will arise from this new space your expression has opened up. When you are able to express the truth of the condition, you begin to see where your resistance actually is. When truth is expressed—even the limited truth!—then the condition is illuminated. It's lifted up.

Now, how you then show up in the world, how your actions or relationships change, is unpredictable. You may find yourself entering a full-time path of service, or you may suddenly notice ways you're already serving that you weren't even aware of. We can't know what will happen, but that's fine! That's just how it works.

It's very true that as you really settle into your true nature, there's often a natural movement that you could call "being of service." But it doesn't show up in some kind of dutiful or righteous way. Rather, the *being of service* I'm talking about is quite selfless. There's no ego in it, no sense of accomplishment or greatness. True service happens quite naturally when there's no longer anyone identified with being of service, and paradoxically, that's also when you'll find *being of service* most fulfilling.

28.

Expression and Inspiration

People often notice that when teaching, I speak a lot about emotion and expression, and they ask why emotion is such a focus of my work. Often I respond, "Well, I grew up as a concert violinist."

I've always been deeply moved by music. When I first learned to read music as a child, I got the score of Tchaikovsky's Violin Concerto in D Major. I loved that piece so much that I would listen to it on my record player and conduct an imaginary orchestra from the score for hours a day. I probably should've become a conductor! But in a way I guess I have. I'm conductor of a symphony of energy.

So I grew up training to be a concert violinist, and my violin was an immensely important vehicle for me throughout my childhood. It was the vehicle for my heart, a profound outlet for my emotional expression. It really got me through my childhood and young adulthood, and kept my emotions alive and fluid under circumstances that might otherwise have led me to shut down. I think in some ways I developed the depth of emotional access I have now by playing that instrument.

My teacher Jean Klein and I had that in common. He was also a concert violinist. We both really loved Bach's Double Violin concerto. I would walk into his room, he would start singing the first violin part, then I would respond by singing the second violin part, and then we'd sing it together until we cracked up laughing. One of the last times I saw Jean, we had planned to finally play it together, but unfortunately he had taken ill, and we never got to do that.

Shinichi Suzuki, the founder of the Suzuki method of learning the violin, said that he taught the violin not to add more violinists to the world, but to develop the heart and improve the character of the music student. I think that was really right on. My study of music helped me in every possible way on my own healing journey and spiritual path, and later in my role as a healer and teacher of others. The way I teach is very much a creative expression for me, in the same way that music was.

Studying music allowed me to develop, very early on, a very refined, sensitized, and multilevel attentiveness. The ability to pay attention is essential for a musician, especially a violinist—the violin is a difficult instrument to play! And because learning the violin requires an enormous amount of practice, I also learned tremendous discipline, which was a great asset to me later on in many different phases of my spiritual journey.

Music also helped me develop a deep ability to listen and to appreciate expression. When I hear someone speaking, it's as if their whole body is a musical instrument through which they're express-ing themselves. I'm aware of very subtle changes in the resonance, vibration, tonality, and timbre of their voice, and as a result what I hear expressed is much more than just the verbal content of the words that are being spoken.

I find that today many people need a lot of help with expression, and so much of my work involves engaging people and encouraging them to speak, to really express where they're at, as honestly and authentically as they can. Speaking in this way is different from simply talking, describing the contents of the mind. This kind of expression is deeper, more full-spectrum. It emerges not from the mind, but from the depth of a person's *being* as they really tune in to where they authentically are, and allow themselves to come forth more fully.

Most people have learned to hide themselves, and to hold them-selves back. They've never been able to speak their truth and be heard in a way that invites their spirit to really shine. When we're not allowed to speak our truth, we hold back our presence. This holding back manifests physically as well, and so often people's physical voices have a very limited range, both in tonality and in volume. There's a kind of constriction there, a held-in-ness, a restriction of their natural movement and energy.

But as someone opens up and relearns how to express, the tonalities and rhythms of their speaking become much more dynamic. Their voices become active, enlivened. They come back to life! When you're awake—when you're truly *alive*—expression becomes a creative act, a creative channeling of your very life force. Now there's music in your speaking, and energy, and light.

Great music and great performances are *inspiring*, and awakening and inspiration are deeply connected. When we stop holding back and allow ourselves to be who we truly are, each of us individually in our uniqueness, we are inspired. We are vibrant, enlivened, spontaneous, and free-flowing. Now we can really live! We can show up fully for our own lives, be present for our own experience, and be available in our relationships with others in ways we might never have been before.

I am endlessly amazed and inspired by the ways people transform, even on a personal level, as they begin to open up and allow themselves to really *be here*, and to show up as who they truly and authentically are.

29.

Mirror of Reality

In addition to my public teaching, I do a lot of private work with individuals, and I find that one of my primary roles is guiding people to have more supportive relationships with themselves. Truly, your relationship with yourself is the most important relationship in your life.

We're often so focused on spiritual growth, on the shift in identity from the limited, personal self to awareness itself. This is of course wonderful, and very important, and obviously I've spent much of this book talking about exactly that. Surprisingly, though, one of the things that really facilitates that shift is becoming aware of how we perceive ourselves and others on a human level. This is part of beginning to notice what I call the *mirror of reality*.

Reality is a mirror, reflecting ourselves right back to us. When sitting silently, we tune in and notice sensations, feelings, thoughts, energies, imagery. We observe the mirror, and see what it offers us to look at, to sense, to listen to, to allow, or to resist.

You can start right now by noticing how you *are* paying attention. Are you allowing this moment, or are you resisting what you're experiencing? Are you being gentle with your body? Even to ask yourself these questions is to begin cultivating a healthier relationship with yourself, which as I've said is absolutely essential. *That* leads to awakening, to the healing and opening of the heart, and also to healthier and more authentic relationships with others.

If you're authentically working on and being really honest with yourself, then any relationship can mirror for you the places you are blocked, or stuck. It's often been observed that it's when you go home to visit your family of origin that you find out how your spiritual practice is really going. When you're walking in some beautiful setting, grooving in presence or connecting deeply with like-minded friends after your meditation group, it's easy to feel wide open and free-flowing, like you've really arrived. Then you fly home to see your parents, and you very quickly find out that maybe you weren't as open as you thought.

Maybe you find instead that you're still very much caught up in reactivity, judgment, and defensiveness in relationship to your family. And if you are, no blame! As difficult as that reactivity may be for you to accept in yourself, it's very helpful to see it and to face it honestly. It's important not to delude yourself about where you're at. Although a nice delusion might help you feel better temporarily, reality won't cooperate for long!

The good news is you don't have to fix, or get rid of, or understand your reactivity or even your delusions. You only need to relax and be the space of awareness that perceives them fully, just as they are.

The purest, most unclouded view emerges naturally as you learn to relax into the full allowing of *what is*, however it is. From that perspective, everything is born each moment. Everything is always new. Everything is discovery—learning, growing, evolving. That endless movement is the miracle and mystery of life itself.

So how can you be continually and completely available to your experience, in such a way that you are guided and transformed? Begin—again!—by simply noticing what you're sensing right now. Notice what you're feeling right now. Let your awareness expand to allow whatever's happening, whether you like it, or don't like it, or are just ambivalent toward it.

And pay attention: When you're looking at someone, what are you actually seeing? When you're listening to someone, what are you actually hearing? Are you identified with being a listener, or is there just listening? Is your mind busy with arguing, judging, comparing, and criticizing, or is there just hearing? Is your body comfortable, and if it isn't, how are you being with that discomfort?

With kindness, gentleness, patience, and forgiveness, continue to question your experience, your thoughts, your conclusions. If you think you know what's happening, stop and ask yourself: "Do I *really* know?" The more you can let yourself *not* know what is happening, the more available you are for transformation. It's in our "knowing" that we keep our identity intact and our defensiveness strong.

The wonder of *being* is beyond knowing. It's beyond analysis, beyond all comparisons and judgments. It's in the open, sensitive realm of the heart that we truly connect as beings. That's the deepest level of relationship. There's no longer "you" and "me." There's just this wonderful, warm, beautiful connectedness—just love. Love doesn't expect anything. It doesn't want anything. It doesn't *mean* anything. It's just open, available, and fully giving and receiving simultaneously in every moment.

30.

"Hell Is Other People"

Human relationships are not always easy. From time to time, I'm sure you have come to a place where you would have agreed with Jean-Paul Sartre when he said, "Hell is other people." That was certainly my reality for much of my life! But not long after I embarked on the spiritual path, I came to understand that "hell" was actually *my reaction to my own perceptions* of other people. That's a very different frame, and it changed the whole dynamic, setting me on a path toward understanding relationships from an entirely new direction.

When you realize that what you're reacting to is not so much other people themselves as your own mental projections of other people, then you can really let go of those reactions. In letting go of your reactions, you are freed from them, and in that freedom you are newly empowered. You may still be triggered by other people, but now you see that your triggers are just information reflected back to you by the mirror of your experience—information that can guide you on this path of discovery.

I'm not saying other people are imaginary or that by awakening you lose all discernment in relation to other people. Obviously there are times you don't want to be with certain people, and it's important to have healthy boundaries in certain situations. You shouldn't remain in an unhealthy or damaging situation, for instance, just because it seems like it would be more accepting and "spiritual" to do so. But when it's workable, your reactions can be grist for the mill, fuel for the fire of your transformation.

For the most part you can—without judgment and without blame—learn to work with your relationships with others as aspects of your relationship with yourself. In doing so, you facilitate the dissolution of the *illusion* of the other—and the illusion of yourself! You let go of all subject–object dynamics and move into a unified field of connection. That's *real* relationship, where there's love that is free of self and other.

In many spiritual teachings, particularly from the non-dual or Buddhist traditions, you'll encounter the term "no-self" as a description of the fruition of the path. That may seem abstract, but it really just means the condition of *no longer being identified*. You still have a personality and personal preferences, but they're not where you live anymore, not where your vibrancy is. You're not contracted around that limited personal self anymore, and therefore no longer so defended. You're just here! You're just open. If two people can be in that open, undefended space together, what's shared between them is the purest kind of love.

We crave that kind of connection, both as human beings and as spiritual beings. It's in our nature to want to be unified, and in truth, that unity is our nature. Unity is not a willed, personal achievement; rather, it's the openness and open-heartedness that is what remains when everything else drops away. That's the relationship you're working on with yourself and simultaneously working on with others.

So your relationships with other people can be helpful mirrors of what's going on in yourself—what you're wanting to control, or change, or push away, or what you're wanting to hold on to or get. *Use* that material instead of just pushing it aside.

◇◇◇◇

On a more personal level, a good relationship is one in which two people are able to communicate in such a way that they understand each other's intentions. That can be challenging because we all have different ways of communicating, different shadings and idiosyncrasies in how we use language and other forms of communication. As a result there's a lot of misunderstanding between people, and also a lot of projection—we tend to make assumptions about what people mean at times that aren't necessarily based in reality.

That's why a big part of the spiritual path is learning to identify and question our assumptions. We try not to assume we really understand what someone else means, or if we do, we learn to *notice* our assumptions and question them. We cultivate awareness of our own internal setup and how we reflexively interpret what we see in others. Anytime you can bring into the space of your own attention your own projection and your own set of meanings, you facilitate intimacy with yourself and with others.

So when interacting with another person, notice where you're at. As the interaction proceeds, do you feel yourself becoming closer to that person, or further away? Feel and sense your body. Notice whether you become physically and energetically more open or more contracted, whether you're available in the interaction or more pulled back and defended. This kind of real-time observation of yourself in relationship can be very, very powerful and instructive. You might call this *spiritual practice in action*.

As always, be gentle with yourself—very gentle. If you're interacting with someone and find yourself contracting, no blame! That's just what's happening, just the natural movement of your emotional and bodily system, and that may even be an appropriate response depending on the situation.

Sometimes you may not want to relate to people at all. If that's the case for you, then just notice that: "I want to hide; I don't want to be around people. I don't want to have to interact," or even, "People bug the hell out of me!" On a human level, we all have limitations in relationship. Sometimes our limitations are irritating, of course, but as you deepen in this process, you learn to take care of them. You learn to accept yourself.

Love, even on a personal level, is 100 percent acceptance. That doesn't mean you can't have issues with how things are—that you can't ask for what you need, or have expectations, resentments, disappointments, and all that. But to expect someone else to change or be different isn't love. Love is when you can see and accept others in all their limitations, just as you see yourself in your own limitations. That's why I emphasize so often the importance of *giving yourself permission to be human*—of accepting yourself just as you are, right now.

31.

Relationship and the Spiritual Process

People involved in the spiritual life often have very strong beliefs about the role of relationship in the spiritual process. Those beliefs can *really* get in the way!

One common belief is that relationship is a distraction or impediment, and that the spiritual aspirant should therefore live a kind of solitary life, only minimally involved with other people. This particular belief is understandable, given that many of the traditions that birthed these practices were actually quite skeptical about the value of relationship. Many people also adhere to a less extreme version of this: the idea that relationship is merely neutral to spirituality—not to be avoided, necessarily, but not particularly important either, and therefore not something to spend much time or effort on.

I'd say both of these perspectives are a bit limited, not to mention outdated. Relationship is immensely important to transformation. Human relationships are fantastic mirrors for illuminating areas of your life where you're still trying to maintain control. Inevitably, other people will really push your buttons, and if you're truly on the path to freedom, then you *welcome* having your buttons pushed. That discomfort shows you, very clearly, where attention is needed in yourself.

Most people go through life trying to avoid difficulty and discomfort, and approach the spiritual process similarly, aiming primarily to minimize suffering and feel better. This is fine at first, and a necessary phase of development for many of us. If you're serious about awakening, though, you'll eventually have to let go of that approach.

Awakening requires the willingness to be continually challenged. If all you want is to remain in your comfort zone, then forget enlightenment. It isn't for you. If you really want freedom, you have to be willing to ride the bronco. You have to be ready to open to what activates you, and what agitates you.

As I've said, the most important relationship in your life is your relationship with yourself. Through a sincere and completely honest relationship with your personal self, you can develop a more direct relationship to your ultimate self, the Big Self that is common to all of us. In relationship to the Big Self, you, in a sense, lose your personal self, and in that loss begin to experience yourself as simply this unified field of awareness that contains and supports and permeates all things.

Now you are in *relationship* with everything. You're no longer separate from anything. From that perspective there is nothing *but* relationship. You are not separate from your friend, your lover, your enemy, or the tree across the street. The energy of awareness infuses everything. Everything is relationship in awareness. That may sound pretty mind-blowing, but I think you'll be surprised to discover just how ordinary it really is.

◇◇◇◇

When it comes to personal connections with other people, your needs will shift over time. Not everyone needs to move to a monastery, but there absolutely may be times and periods in your spiritual process where simplifying your lifestyle, limiting who you hang out with, and spending more time on your own are very helpful, even necessary. I see many people go through these kinds of changes. As you deepen in this process, your social life can go through a real regroup.

This is where paying very close attention to your own process, remaining very tuned in to where you *actually are* in any moment, is essential. You need to cultivate a deep, ongoing listening—to your body, to your energy system, and even to the types of thoughts that appear in your mind—and learn to take care of yourself as needed.

As I said, at times this may mean becoming less social. At different points in your process, you may find that you need to pull back a bit and cultivate more silence and solitude. Eventually, though, what generally happens is that you come full circle. You return fully to your life and all your personal relationships—to your family, your friends, your partner, your children. But now you're returning with a different perspective. Now everything is new.

When you are deeply in relationship with the Big Self, the deeper insight that becomes available, directly and experientially, is that other people are not separate from you yourself. That's not to say you become confused on a human level as to who you are versus who your friend is; you're still able to function as a person. But your experience of the world is now intimate. You're close to everything, but without holding on to anything. You're deeply vulnerable, but without that vulnerability being threatening.

In that space of openness and connectedness, you find profound empathy and compassion for the experience of others. Resistance toward other people falls away. Judgments about them fall away. What now emerges is unconditional love for and profound acceptance of others wherever they're at, however they show up. You find a deep connectedness of heart—of *beingness*—in which there's no need, no expectation, no longing. Each interaction with another person is profound, a simultaneous giving of yourself and complete receiving of the other.

Now of course on a human level, your relationships can change as you deepen in this process. Some may become deeper and more profound, developing in ways you could never have expected, while others may become less intimate than before, or even end. We can't predict how our lives will develop. The truth—as I've said many times throughout this book—is that we don't really know what's going on! We don't know what's going to happen in this life.

So could your relationships change in positive ways? Sure! On the other hand, could some of them end? That's also possible. Anything *could* happen, and if you are honest with yourself, you'll recognize that that's always been the case. The difference is that in the past you might have had a *belief* that things would or should stay the same—that a particular relationship would last forever or develop in the direction you would prefer. But now that your perspective has opened up, you are free of that preconception. You can meet reality as it *actually is* and respond from a place of openness and acceptance.

Sometimes a relationship may end when you really want it to continue. It may be difficult to lose that relationship, but you'll grieve and go through whatever you need to go through. You won't hang on to that regret, or sadness, or resistance to accepting the change at all. You'll be able to go with the flow of the inevitable changes in any relationship, whether those changes are for "better," for "worse," or just unexpected.

As it is in other areas of life, one of the biggest impediments in relationship is our *need to understand*. Many people run into trouble around this point. Their *modus operandi* in terms of how they relate to others, and how they move through life generally, is very much centered around a perceived need to understand what's happening. Further, this strategy gets a lot of support and encouragement from other people. Understanding is generally thought to be a Very Good Thing!

The reality, though, is that you're not always going to understand—and you don't need to! You only need to be here with *what is*, as it is, with honesty and openness of heart. From that place you will respond authentically and effectively, allowing situations to develop on their own, or taking direct action as needed.

The deepest, most authentic relationship is the end of the other and the end of the self. That's love at the highest level—pure connectedness. The truest love is when you're no longer separate at all, but just *being* together, resting in the Heart of Vastness.

32.

Love and Connection: Intimate Relationships

I have a very simple teaching around what are usually called intimate relationships: They either work, or they don't.

More specifically, people are either energetically compatible, or they're not. Relationships between people who are energetically compatible can work, even if those relationships are difficult or challenging. But if you find yourself in a relationship with someone with whom you are not energetically compatible, it's really *not* going to succeed, and there isn't much you can do to force it to.

When my own spiritual process really kicked into gear, I noticed that these kinds of relationships would sometimes just end. In some cases, there seemed to be a straightforward reason, but in others, there was no obvious reason at all. It didn't always have to do with my or the other person's behavior, or a conflict between our personalities, or anything like that. It was more that our lack of energetic compatibility became unavoidable.

This wasn't necessarily a conscious recognition. I didn't suddenly say, "Oh, I see; we're energetically incompatible," and take some kind of intentional action to end the relationship. Rather, it was a natural development and a natural movement. As I became more sensitive to my own energy and that of others, remaining in fundamentally unworkable relationships was no longer an option.

When relationships do end, people often blame themselves or blame the other person. They think things could've been otherwise if they had done this or that differently or the other person had been willing to change or try harder. The truth, though, is that none of that can work when two people's energies are not fundamentally compatible.

That's not to say that you should give up on your relationships at the first sign of difficulty. Difficulties arise between human beings. Relationships do often require work and commitment on a human level. But there needs to be that certain fundamental compatibility on an energetic level for there to be anything to work with in the first place.

At this point you might ask the obvious question: "How can I tell when I'm energetically compatible with someone?" The answer is that you don't need to worry about it. As you deepen in awareness, you become more sensitive to energy, and you'll find yourself seeing these things more and more clearly. You won't necessarily have the thought, *This person and I are energetically compatible*. It will show up more as a tacit recognition and a natural movement from within you to connect more deeply with them.

◇◇◇◇

Another key point in navigating intimate relationship is the recognition that you are ultimately responsible for your own feelings. You may at times experience someone else as being responsible for your feelings, and of course on the surface this can seem to make perfect sense. They behave in a way that triggers you, and you find yourself reacting. Cause and effect seem obvious there, right? But to conceptualize the interaction in this way is to place responsibility for your own reaction on that other person. Now you're requiring them to change what they're doing so you can avoid the experience of getting upset.

We often try to get other people to change in certain ways so we can feel better. But in reality, we have no control over other people. You can certainly ask someone to change their behavior if that behavior seems problematic, but they may or may not comply, or may comply only partly, or temporarily. Ultimately, though, you are fundamentally responsible for your *own* feelings and for taking care of yourself as needed. This means being willing to take care of yourself energetically—to take the clearing work I've been talking about throughout this book into the realm of relationship.

In an intimate relationship, part of that clearing is being able to express your needs, your desires, and even your complaints and resentments in a space where the other person can listen without being triggered—where they can be an open space of just listening to what your experience is.

The quality of this expression is key. It's not about blaming or punishing the other person, or making demands on them. If for instance your partner is behaving in a way that you're experiencing as hurtful, expressing yourself in this way is about just letting them know what you're experiencing, what you feel when they behave that way. "When you speak in that tone, I feel judged." "When you react in that way, I feel attacked." Fundamentally you're offering up the truth of your experience, as authentically and honestly as you can. Now your partner has the opportunity to really understand where you're at, and to respond in whatever way the situation calls for.

In a good relationship, both people can listen to each other and express their needs, desires, and resentments on a regular basis. They can also, obviously, express what they appreciate about each other! But here I'm talking more about clearing things that might be in the way, that might prevent open, honest, and authentic relationship. When communication is both offered and received in a space of openness and receptiveness, two people can get clear with each other pretty easily—and then they can get back to the love.

At times, of course, there may be some things you really *can't* express to your partner, things that would just be too hurtful to them to be helpful. But as these things go unexpressed, some emotional energy or reactivity may build up in your own body, and you need to clear that energy as well. In those cases, I would recommend a version of the expression practice I described earlier in the book.

Sit by yourself in a comfortable position, and as usual, begin with the simple breath. As best you can, allow yourself to relax and center. Notice your feelings. Notice the energy of your body. Notice any tension, any holding, or any agitation or restlessness.

Now imagine your partner in front of you, and as clearly as you can, verbally express whatever it is you need to express. Offer that expression into the space of listening. When you're done, sit quietly for at least a few moments, and tune back in to your body. Notice again how you are feeling. Have your feelings changed or shifted? Are you more relaxed, or less? More open, or less open?

Once you've taken at least a few moments to check in with yourself, try once again offering your expression into the space of listening. You may find it comes out differently this time. You may now be able to access deeper levels of what you need and how you are feeling. I would invite you to take yourself through this process as many times as you need to, to clear what needs to be cleared and to free yourself from it. Let your hurt, anger, frustration, or whatever you're burdened with move and flow out of your nervous system.

In a more general sense, continually doing your own human work, always taking time to clear yourself as needed, will allow you to show up with openness and authenticity in your intimate relationships and all the other relationships in your life as well. In any relationship, whether it's with a partner, friend, family member, or colleague, learning to communicate from a place of openness makes all the difference in the world. It allows both people to grow and allows the relationship to continue to develop.

It also cultivates a deeper intimacy. Many people aren't really authentically themselves in their relationships because they're acting in accord with how they think they should act, or how they think the other person expects or needs them to act. But when you are able to be authentically present with your partner in a shared space of deep listening, then finally you can relax with them, and be who and what you *actually are*.

33.

Looking in the Mirror

We come together with others on this path to be connected, both with each other and with ourselves. We seek out people who are conscious in a way that supports us in exploring and deepening our own consciousness. Even though we may not know each other personally, we find there's nevertheless a sense of familiarity or sensitivity, an awareness that knows itself in the other. There's a kind of union that happens—with ourselves, with each other, and with all things.

Everything is a mirror for you to realize yourself—everything!—and as we've just explored, our relationships and interactions with other people are particularly amazing mirrors. Just being around people, talking with them, observing them—there's so much to learn.

When you awaken—even for just a moment—in that moment you're free of self and other. Everyone experiences those shifts, those moments of awakened consciousness. You're tuned in; you're available; you're connected. And of course when you have those moments, you immediately want more!

That's why you're here, now, on this amazing path to awakening. You're developing that availability, deepening that connection. The path can be difficult at times and very challenging to stick with, and yet you are sticking with it. You're hanging in there. So give yourself some well-deserved gratitude for the hard work and commitment that have kept you going this far.

Your heart needs gratitude. It needs appreciation and tenderness. It needs to feel and also express appreciation—not just as some platitude, but deeply, sincerely. So cultivate your heart. Cultivate love for yourself, appreciation for yourself. Don't make the mistake of focusing solely on your brokenness and limitations. Rather, focus on the beauty of who you are and the beauty of who others are.

Now you'll start appreciating people and loving them, despite their flaws and failures, their missteps and screw-ups. You'll love everyone, profoundly, regardless of how they're able to show up. That's the gift of freedom. That's the ultimate relationship. Everyone is in your heart. Now you see that even the things about others that really trigger you only reflect things you can't accept or sometimes even see in yourself. Each of us has it all. From the darkest of the dark to the brightest of the bright, we each have the full spectrum. That's what it is to be human.

We're all always working with our difficult relationships, whether with people presently in our lives or those in our past whose effect on us continues even now. I've been working on this my whole life—my own family of origin was a battleground! There's no end to this work, but it will transform you. So embrace it. Use it. Relationship is where our passion is, and anywhere there's that much juice, there's enormous possibility for transformation.

34.

The Freedom Equation

Let's switch gears! Imagine you're in algebra class. There's a big blackboard in the front of the room with the word "Freedom" written on it. Underneath it in parentheses, maybe add your own choice of words—enlightenment, peace, happiness, fulfillment, liberation, salvation.

If asked to suggest a formula for freedom, most people would say something like "$a + b =$ freedom." But I'm going to give you the real formula right now:

One minus one equals freedom.

Returning to zero, we are everything and nothing simultaneously. We are freedom, form, and emptiness—relative and absolute—integrated. *One minus one.*

Whatever you have, give it away. Whatever you're holding on to, let go of it. Return to zero—to openness, to clarity. Let your mind become a crystal clear mirror, free of debris. Now you are what you see. You are what you feel. You are connected.

◇◇◇◇

Everyone's path is unique. Each of us has to find out how, in our own experience, to allow *one minus one* to happen. This is the point of something as basic and valuable as mindfulness practice. Bringing attention to what's arising, to what's present in our experience, can allow each individual to *find out how* to bring awareness to what's perceived in such a way that the perceiver can evaporate.

That doesn't mean we need to cultivate an expectation or desire that the perceiver should evaporate; we only need to recognize that a certain way of giving attention produces *one minus one*. This happens not through any effort or belief on our part, but simply because it is our very nature to dissolve, just as an ice cube dropped into a glass of warm water will slowly return to its original nature. Freedom is a natural unfolding of consciousness. By sitting still, breathing, and paying attention in a certain way, consciousness is cultivated.

Of course consciousness has many names. Awareness, presence, beingness, even God or the Divine—these are different ways of speaking about consciousness, subtly different descriptions of the many ways consciousness is experienced. But ultimately these terms all refer to the same mysterious energy—this vibrant, aware life force that is what we fundamentally are. Everything we experience arises from this energy.

Even thought is energy. In discussions of spirituality, thought is often considered an impediment because it's so often involved in struggling with or resisting *what is*—trying to understand it or figure it out, or defending some belief or set of ideas. That kind of thinking can exacerbate suffering and sometimes even create it. And yet there's another realm where thought is magnificent, creative, and liberating.

One of the most obvious and usually unconscious areas is speaking. We're talking all the time! We're communicating now more than ever—e-mailing, texting, and all the many other ways we connect verbally with each other. When speaking, we very often get caught up in our thinking, but that doesn't have to be the case. We are expressive beings, and as I've suggested in earlier chapters, expression can be a vehicle for liberation.

Often we've been conditioned to fit in, and belong, and live up to others' expectations or our own, and so we've restricted our authentic natures, constricted our natural ability to express our-selves. Expression can be so powerful. When we allow it to arise from the space of awareness, expression can open our heart and open our being.

So whether you're giving attention to body, heart, energy, pres-ence, or even the mind, any of them can reveal, in any moment, an opportunity for *one minus one* to happen. But it's also important to understand that we can't control or manipulate transformation. *One minus one* happens by itself—we don't make it happen. There's no control or manipulation in it. Freedom is a seed that germinates by itself, completely naturally. We are seeds that *have* germinated.

Every moment of freedom is a moment of awe. How often do we stop and really look at what's in front of us? Our very existence is an inexplicable and unknowable miracle. So stop and *notice* that miracle. Otherwise you're *doing* life—being somebody, getting somewhere—rather than *being* life. But life itself is the great teacher, and what's happening for you in *every moment* is the teaching. So stop, relax, and let that teaching in.

In any moment you can ask yourself, "What is it going to take, right now, for me to *be here* 100 percent—open, available, receptive, and alive?" Ask the question into the space of awareness, and maybe something will be given to you in that moment—some insight, guid-ance, or revelation, or maybe just an overwhelming sense of relief that you took that one second to stop. Maybe then you'll take another second—and then many more seconds!

I often lead retreats that last several days, a week, or more, and the number one complaint that I hear about them is that they have to end! But the truth is, they don't end. The retreat goes with you. This teaching does too. This teaching *is* you, right now and always. When you see the radiance of another—when you encounter the transmission of a teacher or teaching—what you're really seeing is your own true self reflected. When you're feeling love, you're giving and receiving your own true heart.

We are happiest and most fulfilled as human beings when we are in that unified space of unconditional love, giving and receiving open-heartedly. Everyone has had at least moments of that fullness, that fulfillment, and of course we all want to live there all the time. Because that's home! Our internal guidance system knows that's the big zero, the true fullness of being—the *one minus one*.

It's amazing that through something as basic as *simply paying attention*, this presence and aliveness that you are can come to the foreground. Awakening is available right here, right now. You need only stop trying and surrender to it, give yourself to it, and allow yourself to be brought home to be nurtured, loved, and fulfilled unconditionally. Because, you know, trying to get fulfilled conditionally is a mixed bag! You win some; you lose some. But it's nice to know that what you can *truly* rely on, what you can truly trust, is not outside of yourself at all.

◇◇◇◇

If you want to remember anything I've said in this book, make it this: *Just be right here.* Give yourself permission to be right here. Whatever it takes to be right here—forgiveness, compassion, patience, tenderness—allow yourself to receive it, and then listen to the teaching in the sound of silence, in the alive stillness.

Awakening happens by itself. The only thing we're really learning here is how to *allow* it to happen. Take a moment to really let that in. I think you'll find it lifts the burden of being responsible for your spiritual progress from your shoulders, giving you a whole different perspective on what responsibility really means. Just bringing awareness to *what is*, allowing *what is* to be in awareness, you might say that's a kind of effortless responsibility. Otherwise we get caught up in doing it, managing it, orchestrating it.

The secret is in allowing yourself to discover what *being awareness* is, what *being presence* is, and then discovering it over and over and over again, and importantly, *letting what happens, happen*—without grasping, or holding on to, or trying to shape your experience. Any attempt to grasp after or hold on to awakening only pushes it into the background.

As human beings we're so programmed to survive, to seek comfort and avoid pain, and so it's difficult for us to trust that the process is happening and to just let that awareness take us. But eventually we do begin to learn, and gradually we realize that this presence is a kind of force field, and that every cell in our body can dissolve into that field.

Awakening is the enlivening of the body, the enlivening of the mind—and the discovery and embrace of a vibrant aliveness of *being.*

35.

Transmission: The Deepest Inheritance

Have you ever considered that in a very real sense you're walking around with your ancestors? Think of all the countless human beings in the past who came together and whose lives and actions resulted in your being here, right now, in the body you inhabit.

Most of us don't usually consider the fact that we have inherited this life, that it's been, in a sense, given to us. There's an old Zen koan that asks, "What did your face look like before your parents were born?" I'm going to spoil it for you: *It was awareness itself.* There has always been this awareness, this presence—this *aliveness*. We can't wrap our minds around it. We can't wrap our thoughts around it. And yet it is our deepest inheritance.

When we examine ourselves from a conventional perspective, we often look at the characteristics we've inherited from our parents—our genetics; our personality structures; our cultural, religious, and familial conditioning. We all live with that conditional inheritance or programming, the consequences of those many, many relationships and interactions. When that programming becomes limiting, if we're paying close attention, we begin to realize that it is the root of so much of our suffering. So we're drawn here, to the path of awakening, and here there's an inheritance happening as well.

Spiritual transmission is also the passing on of an inheritance. That's why spiritual traditions often talk about "lineage," and have rituals like the passing on of the robe and the bowl. In its most authentic sense, "lineage" is just a formal recognition of the connection that's always been there anyway. The rituals acknowledge, symbolically, that you've discovered that inheritance, that ever-present connection; that you've recognized and brought it into consciousness; and that the spiritual path has become the reality of your life.

I've been fortunate to have many profound teachers in this life. What made those relationships work was that I was deeply and profoundly in love with those people. That love was mutual, but it also wasn't personal. It was what I call falling in love at the high level. By that I mean finding out what it means to be unguarded, undefended—to be open, unidentified, free of any self that even needs defending. Once that kind of love is there, then it's always there, whether that relationship continues on a personal level or not. Even with my teachers who have moved on from this life, that connection remains alive.

Spiritual teaching is at its purest when there are no longer two people involved. When there are no longer self and other—and therefore no "teacher" and no "student"—what's left is just this energetic connectedness, and then true teaching takes place. Prior to that, you as a student are still looking for something outside of yourself, maybe some reassurance or acknowledgment, or you're wanting the teacher to be someone who's going to help you, or give you the answer, or fix you, or take care of you.

That's not to say there's no place for wanting and needing and getting those things. Our human needs are important and shouldn't be denied or overlooked. But at the higher level, you let go of the personal and become completely tender, completely open. You let down your guard, and notice what's *actually here* right now when you're no longer being somebody, when you're no longer identified.

So I'm not here to teach you. Rather, I'm here to support you in discovering this so-called path for yourself. That support is offered energetically—it's not an intellectual process. The intellect can play a part in it, obviously, because we are thinking beings, and of course spiritual guidance is often conveyed verbally (for instance, the words you're reading now). But the intellect must ultimately be subservient to the deeper process we're engaged in here. The mind is not the dominating factor in this classroom.

What leads us here to this path is not the intellect, but rather our inner truth, our inner wisdom. The wisdom of the Vast Heart— that's the real teacher. I sometimes avoid even using the word "teacher" since it can imply someone who knows something you don't and from whom you need to acquire that knowledge. But in truth this wisdom is already yours. You already have it. It's *what you already are.*

So how can you become more available to what you already are? Deeply, truly available? By *letting it happen.* Not by knowing what's happening or understanding, but by simply being available, and letting *it* happen. As that availability grows in you, your perception changes, and your understanding changes. Even how you communicate changes. And then you find yourself in this wonderful realm of intimacy, of connection—of the Big Heart.

So take a moment right now to *tune in* to your experience, and ask yourself: How am I, right now? What's present for me, right now? Am I fully here, or am I holding back? Am I distracted, or am I present? Is my body at peace, or is there discomfort or contraction?

Notice what happens when you ask yourself these questions. Notice also how it feels to be listened to, even by yourself! Something happens when we're listened to—something begins to open. Notice that opening. Rest your attention in that opening. *Be* that opening. *Let it happen.*

Our heart naturally wants to open. Our being naturally wants to shine. It's just how we are; it's just *what* we are. You are already that which you seek. You are already free, even if it's not your experience and you don't yet believe it. So notice what's calling for your attention right now. Listen deeply, feel deeply—and notice what happens when you do.

In my work I'm deeply blessed to meet many people who are really, deeply finding out how this miraculous transformational healing process works. It's nice to be able to share that with everyone and an amazing privilege to be able to support people in *directly experiencing* this truth so that they can trust, more and more, that it's real, and that the mystery of transformation is alive in them.

Let's face it: Life *is* a mystery. We really don't have a clue! We may have some basic, practical understanding of how to manage our human affairs and keep ourselves alive, but where this life comes from and what it actually is, we have no idea. At first, acknowledging that can be overwhelming and scary, but as we gradually deepen into awareness, we find that *not knowing* is ultimately a source of great relief.

As we come to understand the nature of this path, we find that we're really *not* looking for information or for some final answer to our spiritual questions. Rather, we're learning to *live* the question, to rest in the mystery of life itself. That mystery is our home, our resting place. That's why spirituality is often called "mysticism," but never "answerism"!

Many of us enter the spiritual path with the idea that we'll eventually achieve a kind of permanent high, an endless altered state. But as we rest ever more deeply in *not knowing* and gradually let go of our ideas and expectations, what actually happens is that mystical reality becomes our ordinary reality—and yet always remains a mystery.

36.

Connected in the Big Heart

Take another moment to stop, relax, and let yourself hang out for a bit. Let go of the past, and let go of the future. Let go of anticipation, of expectation. Let go, even if for just this moment, of the *need to know*. Let that weight come off your heart. Needing to know is a real burden! "Where are we? What's going on? When will we get there? How will we know?"

Isn't it lovely just to be without all that—to just rest and enjoy, without all that baggage weighing you down? You're open, free of resistance, free of reactivity. No longer stuck on the treadmill of the mind, you're just open-minded, open-hearted, open-*bodied*. Open in *being*. Just open! It's so simple. Even labeling it simple is too complicated.

As I said at the very beginning of this book, what we're all really looking for is just to be happy. That's the opportunity of awakening—to be happy and fulfilled *right now*. Not in the next life or when all the right circumstances finally line up, but right here. Right now. Awakening—happiness!—is what we are, fundamentally. Beneath all our filters and veils and roles, we're just *here*. We're just *being*. Nothing is missing. Nothing is lacking. Nothing needs to be fixed, figured out, gotten rid of, or held on to.

In relaxing, we are ever more open to the transmission of the truth—of our own deep inheritance, our very nature itself. Transmission is not an intellectual process, a conveying of information. Rather, it is simply the direct recognition that we are *all* this energy, all this radiant presence.

Again, it's just not the case that someone else has the presence and you don't, and you need to get it from them. Even so, in the connection with someone who is living from that openness—a so-called "teacher"—you can find a unique kind of support, a kind of mirroring effect. In that connection, the dust clears, and your own brightness is reflected back to you.

So open to this energy, this light, and enjoy its radiance. It's like sunbathing on a beautiful day. It feels good! So enjoy the light that you are. As far as I'm concerned, we're always celebrating that light, and it's such a joy to celebrate it with you, and to just *be here*.

In person I sometimes hesitate to use words because words can so easily bring us up into our head, when where we really want to be is in our heart. That's the real eventual blooming in this process of awakening—experiencing not only the light, but also the deep connectedness of the Heart of Vastness. I know it can be a difficult and sometimes overwhelming journey, but together we can find the deep nurturing and support that can carry us to the fruition of this path.

Transmission is happening whether we communicate directly or not. It happens in the words and in the silence. If you're at a place where awareness is forefront in your experience, then these words are not really necessary, so just let them be in the background. If on the other hand you're caught in anticipation: "What's he going to say next?" or confusion: "What does he mean by that?" then see if you can just notice that anticipation or confusion. Notice it, and let it be there. Watch what it does.

Now see if you can notice the one who is noticing. Become aware of the space within which noticing is happening. Even if there is still anticipation or confusion, now you see that it too is arising within that space. It's not *you* who is anticipating or confused—anticipation and confusion are just energies, movements within the weather system of your human organism.

Now you begin to see that what you truly are is just this space, this openness—this aliveness. It's so simple; it's not even a concept—it's preconceptual. So it's even pre-simple! Of course, when you get to the pre-simple, you open up the entire universe, which might normally seem extremely complex. But at that point you're no longer thinking about it because your mind is completely blown.

◇◇◇◇

The path is through the heart. Often the mind seems like a problem, always trying to understand and control. But it's important to offer the mind some love and acceptance too. It's doing the best it can! It's trying to protect you and take care of you the only way it knows how. As you deepen in this process, though, gradually the mind relaxes and assumes a more subordinate position. It becomes a helpful guide, a trusting ally.

Spiritual transformation happens by itself in a mysterious realm that has nothing to do with our personal will. It's already happening; it's already *happened*. This is all true! But it's also very important to make sure we're not rejecting anything in ourselves or marginalizing anything in our human experience, pushing away things we may not like. True realization encompasses our complete human experience. It is the ocean that includes everything—the starfish and the jellyfish and the dolphins, but also the garbage and pollution and oil slicks.

One of the great gifts of realization is moving completely out of the realm of being a believer and into the realm of being an explorer and a discoverer, which is a lot more fun and a heck of a lot more interesting. To be a discoverer is to be alive, curious, and continually surprised. To be a believer is to be stiff and crusty, shut down, and threatened. Which one sounds better to you?

The choice is yours, in every moment.

37.

The Healer's Path

In the late 1970s I left the monastery and began a new phase of life as a hands-on healer. After several years of intensive training, I went into private practice as a teacher and practitioner of the Alexander Technique.

I'd learned about Frederick Matthias Alexander's work when I sought help for back pain I experienced during my Zen training. I'd had a back injury when I was eighteen, which I later realized had left me with very strong patterns of tension in my body that didn't go away even after my back was mostly physically healed. I realized that I had to bring awareness to those protective dynamics in order to allow them to open up and release the energy that was being held there.

The Alexander Technique, if you're not familiar with it, is a very refined body awareness training, a kind of inner energy work. I found it to be very compatible with my meditation, as well as with my yoga, tai chi, and the other practices I studied. It's about bringing aware-ness into the physical body, whether in movement or in stillness. It helped me become much more sensitive to the energies and needs of my own body, and so I was moved to learn more and to seek out training with early practitioners like Frank Ottiwell, Marjorie Barstow, and others.

When I began my private practice, I quickly found myself working with many people in the performing arts world. Because of my own background as a violinist, I very much understood the physical challenges of being a musician and the wear and tear on the body that's unavoidable when practicing the craft of playing an instrument at a high level. I worked with numerous dancers and athletes as well, many of whom had very similar issues.

When I began working with clients, I soon found that I was experiencing many of their bodily issues in my own body. For instance, a ballet dancer came in for a session. As I worked on him, I began having some discomfort in my right leg, and at some point during the session he said, "Oh, I forgot to tell you that I injured my right leg the other day." That kind of thing happened all the time, and the cumulative effects became difficult to manage. It took me about a year of private practice to begin to understand what was happening and to figure out how to work with it in a way that made it possible for me to continue.

What I discovered is really the root of the clearing and grounding work I've described in this book. I had to learn to be a channel through which people's energy flowed rather than a receptacle in which it collected. I also found that when I put my hands on someone, my attention had to be in that same part of my own body—I actually had to work on my own body while working on theirs.

Although before this I was familiar with spiritual teachings about oneness, unity, and so on, it was only then that I really began to understand viscerally and practically that even on a human level we are not separate at all. Our energy systems are one. That's what makes empathy possible. You feel for another person, you empathize with them, only to the extent that you're open to them energetically. Feeling someone else's feelings? That sounds impossible, right? And yet, we all experience it. Whether we conceptualize it that way or not, we've all had that experience.

Later, when I trained others as healers, this was one of the main things I tried to convey. Whether you're a bodyworker, a hands-on healer, or even a therapist, it's very important to be able to clear yourself; otherwise, you're going to take on other people's energies and burn yourself out. You need to be a channel, not a receptacle; a river, not a lake. You have to allow energy to flow through and out rather than letting it build up in you.

It's also very important not to *identify* as a healer. I emphasized to people I was training that if they for one moment thought they were working on someone else, they were already in the way of the process. If you take on the *identity* of being a healer, you're not really a healer. Instead you're someone "doing" healing, someone trying to heal someone else. An authentic healer is selfless, free of any sense of ownership or responsibility for the healing that flows through them.

The same is true of teaching. Someone who takes on the *identity* of being a spiritual teacher is not really a spiritual teacher because that very identity gets in the way of the teaching. For an authentic spiritual teacher, there is no thought, feeling, or orientation of "being a teacher." There's no sense of specialness or of being a person who has something others don't—in fact there's no sense of being a person at all. In the interaction with others, there is simply this open, unified field of connection, of verbal and nonverbal communication.

We all have moments of selflessness, when we're "in the zone," so to speak. It can happen while surfing, or running, or playing music, or just walking in nature. Suddenly experience is so completely enveloping that there is no *you* anymore. There's no longer any identification with anything, no one left *to* identify with anything.

◇◇◇◇

The spiritual journey and the healing journey are not separate, but are really just different aspects of, or perspectives on, one unified movement toward openness. I've said many times that true spirituality is not about transcending the human, but rather about becoming *fully* human. Many people want to leave their humanity behind because they associate the human experience with suffering. Suffering is a drag, right? Even healing, getting better, is difficult. And yet that's the progression that happens: first healing, then transformation, and then finally integration.

But despite how that may sound, the spiritual process is not linear. Awakening is not a residence, not a destination at the end of a clear path. Rather, it's constant fluidity, endless movement in all directions. Spiritual development is an alive ecosystem of change and transformation. As you come to understand this, you begin to have more compassion for yourself, more acceptance of your own struggles. Now you can stop judging yourself and beating yourself up for your limitations. Now you can allow yourself, finally, to just be human.

38.

The Light That You Are

Our human bodies are fragile, with so many weaknesses and limitations. We get ill. We get injured. We get older, with all the changes that aging brings. But even though your body may at times be profoundly compromised, that will not in any way obscure the light that you are. That doesn't mean that being compromised will be pleasant, but interestingly, it can in some ways bring the light more to the forefront. When you're physically impaired, you're forced to pay attention in a way you might not otherwise. In recent years I've come to understand this very deeply in a way I didn't before.

A few years ago I had major surgery. After the first few days, when I was finally able to walk around the ward in my hospital gown with my walker, I felt like I was back in the monastery doing my walking meditation. It was very difficult to walk and very difficult to breathe, and there was a lot going on around me. There were all the other patients there, the staff running around, and so on. But in that moment, *that* was what was happening. That was what was appearing in the mirror of reality. Just like *this* is what's happening, right now. *Whatever* is happening, there is only *this*. Only now.

The more you open to the deeper presence that you are, the more you can be fully present with *whatever* needs your attention, loving tenderness, and care, however difficult or challenging that might be. That's really the point of this practice, this path. The purpose of life is to be fully here, fully *alive*, regardless of whatever limits or challenges we may face.

So, whatever is present for you right now, are you available simply to be here with what's happening? Maybe you're feeling really open, really connected to presence and oneness. It's easy to be available to that, right? But even if you're feeling uncomfortable, agitated, or unhappy, or you're in pain or distress, I invite you to allow that too. Just allow it to happen, to be exactly what it is, and notice if there's any resistance to it in yourself.

Listen deeply to your body, your emotions, your energy system, and notice the difference, kinesthetically, between resistance and allowing. If there is resistance, notice that there's also the awareness of that resistance, the space within which it arises. In that space, there's no judgment about the resistance. There's no resistance to the resistance, as it were.

You might think, *I shouldn't have resistance. I should be at peace. What's wrong with me?* Well, if you're not at peace, then you're not. That's what's *actually happening.* Even if you're agitated or in turmoil, there is nevertheless a space that *allows* that to be happening—a space that, you might say, "accepts" it. I often use the word "accept" in quotes because the term could imply an agreement with what's happening, as in psychological acceptance. But the acceptance I'm referring to is not psychological, but rather simply the pure awareness of the resistance, without any opinion or position, without any conclusions or comparisons.

What I'm suggesting is not in the realm of cognitive processing at all, not the result of comparing and concluding, but rather direct experience, the end of or the disappearance of the filter of the personal self. You might say there's a merging of experience with consciousness—a true intimacy of being. There's no longer any separation at all; it's a oneness of energy, of heart, of being. There is no longer a *someone* in the way. Whether you realize it or not, you have already had many moments of that intimacy. It's natural to be what you truly are—energy, light, and space. And love! The love of the Big Heart.

Being awake is our natural condition. What is it that's always present regardless of where you are or what's happening around you?

150

Only this awakeness, this radiant presence, the alive space of vastness. This ease of being is available to you right now. In this very moment you can allow the natural letting go of your body and mind and heart to happen. You can relax. You can be at ease.

Being at ease is a bit counter-instinctual. We instinctively feel pushed to seek and to strive, to seek comfort and protection, to defend ourselves. But true ease of being needs no guarding, no defense. There's no one to protect, nothing to hold on to anymore. There's just open availability of attention, closeness—the intimacy of connectedness.

◇◇◇◇

I crave ease, but every time I get close to it, something happens that seems to be out of my control, and then that peace is gone.

It sounds like you're trying make peace happen. The truth, though, is that you can't move toward ease. All you can do is bring awareness to where you *actually are* in this moment. Any attempt to *get* peace will only create tension internally, subtly pushing that peace away.

But right now, you're here. You're present in this moment. Can you let yourself just *be* right here? Notice if you're trying to get something from this moment, trying to make it a certain way, or holding onto something about it that you like. Now take a step back, and just *notice* that trying. *That's* where you want to put your attention.

Ironically, if you focus on the ease, you'll actually get caught in the trying. You'll be identified with the trying. So simply *notice* the trying, and bring awareness to the *one* who is trying, the person who's desperate for that ease and is trying so hard to get it. There's no blame for that, no judgment. You're human, and that's just how humans are conditioned to operate. But if you can make that dynamic conscious, you'll find it will begin to dissolve by itself.

◇◇◇◇

I get so angry with myself because I can't seem to get this. I feel responsible for my own suffering.

If you find yourself getting frustrated, then try offering yourself a little forgiveness: "I'm sorry. I'm sorry I'm so angry, destructive, frustrated. Please forgive me." That will help your heart open. You don't want to live at war with yourself, do you? So make peace. Be nice to yourself. Have some compassion for your own suffering. See how that works.

I invite you now to just be in your body—to just be here right now. See if you can let go even of these words. We're just meeting each other, right here, through these words.

The quality of wanting has a forward motion to it. And that's fine! No blame, no judgment. But that forward motion can prevent us from being conscious of this presence, this ease that's always available to us if we're available to it. As soon as you let go and really drop into being here, the flower of that ease will bloom naturally.

39.

The Deepest Embrace

Despite its many challenges—and sometimes because of them—the body is a beautiful feedback system. In my own spiritual journey, my body was—and still is!—a great teacher, and as I've said, it very much guided me onto the healer's path. The body can of course be frustrating sometimes, depending on what your particular body goes through. Of course the mind can be frustrating as well, as can the emotions, but gradually you come to understand more and more directly that these are all just aspects of one unified system.

If you're familiar with traditional non-dual spiritual teachings, you've no doubt encountered the very pure teaching, "You are not the body; you are not your mind; you are not your feelings; you are pure consciousness." From an absolute perspective, that's quite true, and for many people, encountering that teaching is vital at a certain point in their spiritual development. But to realize that is only the beginning.

We are consciousness itself, but as consciousness we become sensitive to the natural processes of our lives. We open to the intuitive, to the guidance that is always present, and one of the many ways guidance comes to us is through the body. Openness allows us to simply let our body go through what it goes through and let our mind go through what it goes through based on our conditioning.

As we become more available to our experience, as we learn to allow ourselves to be guided, then letting go happens by itself. So instead of asking, "How can I let go?" instead try, "How can I be available for *letting go* to happen?" That may be the only question you need to ask.

So how is your body, right now? Is it relaxed and calm, or is it tense or sore? Is it complaining? Let's face it, if the body is not happy, it lets you know. It communicates that unhappiness with sensations and feelings. People sometimes think that after awakening they'll be rid of those kinds of troublesome feelings and sensations, that they'll somehow bypass the less pleasant aspects of the human experience. But that's actually pretty ridiculous.

Through awakening we become *truly* human; we deeply and fully embrace the rich, painful, blissful, temporary, ever-changing human experience. What we find in awakening is true compassion for our humanity because ultimately, what other choice do we have? It's either resist or love.

◇◇◇◇

I've been having a difficult time lately. I've been feeling very dense and burdened.

I would invite you to bring gentle attention to that which is feeling dense and burdened. Allow presence to emerge and do its work. Awareness is the saving grace that is always here to support us, however we feel or whatever we happen to be going through.

◇◇◇◇

I do feel that presence, more and more. But it doesn't make the pain go away.

Pain has its own cycle, its own gestation period, and that cycle needs to play out fully. So what's really important to notice is whether there's anything holding the pain back, or getting in the way of the cycle completing itself. We often create unconscious protective mechanisms that hold in our pain. These mechanisms can be very subtle, but the light of awareness will bring them into a kind of vivid relief, and you'll begin to notice their functioning in a way that you might not have been able to before.

Let yourself deepen, as you are right now, into awareness itself, and then notice what's sticking out. Notice the edges, the tightness, whatever it is, however it shows up. This is what's called *practice*. Some people have an aversion to that word, but when you understand it in the context of awareness, "practice" is actually essential for liberation.

As you tune in more deeply, your pain and grief will begin to emerge. Not just grief around your current situation, but also older grief, older pain that's very deep, from long, long ago. Who knows how far back our unconscious goes, how much old pain we're carrying? When you awaken, you'll find out. You'll release it all, you'll process it all, and ultimately you'll recycle it all. All the garbage, all the pain, will be transmuted into free-flowing energy.

So just feel whatever is there—the pain, the grief, the sadness, the hurt—and give yourself some sympathy, some love. You're open. You're beautiful. And you're letting it all go now, gradually but inevitably. You can't push this river, but when you can see how *letting go* works, you begin to become more skilled at trusting this process and allowing it to flow naturally.

We've learned to resist nature. There's no need to blame ourselves for that—we needed to survive, and for most of us the only way we could do that was to shut down and protect ourselves by resisting, by armoring, by denying. But now we have the deep, profound support of awareness, and shutting down is no longer necessary. We can finally come back and finish all the old, unfinished business of our human conditioning.

Always remember that it's *okay* to have that human condition. Liberation is not limited by our difficulties on the human level. You can be working through trauma, for instance, or struggling with physical illness, and still be deeply, completely liberated and utterly free and happy. At the human level we'll always be flawed and imperfect, and yet in that very imperfection we *are* perfect.

40.

Lighten Your Load

See if you can allow yourself to arrive as fully as you can right now. Just here. With whatever you're sensing, whatever you're feeling. Whatever's happening in your mind, your body, your heart, or your energy field. If you need to, bring attention to your breath to help you calm down and become more relaxed.

If you find yourself opening, expanding, releasing—then allow that expansion. If on the other hand you find yourself uncomfortable and resistant, struggling with your mind, your body, or your heart, then allow *that*—but also bring in some compassion for yourself, some tenderness, some reassurance and support. Be patient with yourself.

Many of us are very hard on ourselves, and who can blame us? We live in a competitive, judgmental world. We've been conditioned to compare ourselves to others—to put ourselves down and think poorly of ourselves and our efforts. In my private practice I'm constantly working with individuals who feel bad about where they are. "I've been meditating all these years, I've gone to so many retreats, and I'm still stuck. What's wrong with me?"

As you open more and more into this presence that you are, you'll find it illuminates the dark. It creates an incredible space of expansion, but that same space also allows what has been hidden in the unconscious to bubble up into view. Some people find this frustrating. As you initially learn to relax into awareness, the experience is often wonderful and a great relief. But then up from the depths comes all this uncomfortable material—and the more you allow yourself to relax, the more of this awful stuff comes up! You may think you're doing something wrong or that your spiritual process has gone off the rails somehow.

But you're not doing anything wrong. You *can't* do anything wrong, not really, not when it comes to becoming free. Awakening is a continual dismantling of your beliefs and ideas about how things should be going and how you should be developing. Of course you begin the process with a particular frame, a particular perspective; that's just how the mind works. But ultimately you'll move beyond your expectations.

There are always options when it comes to how you perceive what's happening. So I would invite you, just for fun, to notice what your attitude is about anything at all that comes up—a person, a situation, what she said, what he did. Notice your reactions, your feelings, your responses. And then ask yourself: "Is there another perspective I could have about this?"

As always, pay close attention to how you feel. Does this questioning open you up or make you feel more contracted? Real questioning *will* open you up. If you are instead feeling more contracted, then question *how* you are questioning. Question even the attitude or perspective you have about questioning your attitudes and perspectives!

When you do open up, when you have more space, then you can breathe and feel better. That's what you need. That's what we're all looking for. That spaciousness is freedom itself. When we taste that truth, then naturally we long for more of it. We don't want to feel contracted, compressed, and defended. We want to be open, alive, and curious. We want to enjoy the moment, if we can. Otherwise, what's the point of this life?

Of course there are times in our lives that are challenging, and are very, very difficult. And yet, with this bigger perspective we can find our way even then, despite all that adversity and difficulty.

The fundamental teaching, the guiding principle, is simply to rest as your own true nature. Whether you're aware of that nature or not, it is, always has been, and always will be what you are. Belief has nothing to do with it. Your efforts have nothing to do with it. It is already here, fully present, right now. It is already *what you are.*

Your perception, your experience of that true nature, may be blocked. Some internal resistance may be preventing you from perceiving it. So whatever is holding back your perception, give *that* your attention. I can promise you that holding wants to move. Your being naturally wants to open, naturally wants to release, relax, and let go.

So continually inquire into your own experience, and in each and every moment, find out how to lighten your load. If forgetting everything you know does the trick, fine! But maybe you also need to give loving attention to some pain in your body. Maybe you need to tend to some difficult feelings—some grief, sadness, irritation, or frustration.

Whatever is happening, now and anytime, see if you can bring yourself back to a place where there's a little more *allowing.* Maybe even give yourself some explicit guidance: "Okay, let's do a nice long inhale, and a nice long exhale. Let's *just calm down.*" Or maybe you just lie down, or stand in the sun for a moment, or have your hand held by a friend. Whatever you need, let yourself have it.

The other important ingredient is to give yourself some appreciation. Give yourself some gratitude for all your hard efforts. Even if you're struggling, or you're not where you want to be or where you think you should be, just tell yourself, "I love and appreciate you anyway. I know you're really trying." We all need to know that we're appreciated and loved, and our essence is unconditional love and acceptance. Let it continually heal you, and nourish you, and guide you.

If some of what I'm saying doesn't make any sense to you or is not yet your experience, then let me simplify it in a different way. I would say forget these words and just focus on your body and on your breath. Allow yourself to find a place of stillness that is comfortable and where you can really begin to relax. Find some ease. Even if for just a little while, let go of trying. Let go of striving. Very gently bring awareness to anything in you that's holding back. Anything that's resisting. Any fear, or insecurity, or reluctance.

Allow yourself to dissolve in the space awareness creates. When there's no longer anything holding you back, what's left is just love, and there's no end to how much you can love. The more you give, the more you receive. That's what transmission is. As you connect into the light and your separate self dissolves, you make that light available to everyone.

So let yourself dissolve. Let yourself be taken. Fall back into the arms of the infinite.

41.

Meditation: Going Deeper

As you may have discovered by now, silent sitting can be a bit of an adjustment in relation to our usual ways of operating in this life. Most of us are so busy. We're always active, always running from one thing to the next. So stopping, resting in concentrated stillness, does take some adjustment, especially at first. Sitting quietly, you may find yourself feeling restless, impatient, or irritated. You may feel uncomfortable or bored, or anxious that something, somewhere, is not being done.

So I invite you to hang in there. Let your experience be what it is, and let it develop as it will, even if—maybe especially if—it's not what you expected or not how you think it should be. Notice any discomfort or anxiety, and notice also any conclusions you may be drawing about your experience—any judgments or assumptions about how you're doing, whether you're doing it right, or even whether you want to be doing it at all. If you find yourself feeling contracted, or tight, or tense, step back and just let that feeling be there. Watch that feeling. Listen to it.

As you gradually settle into and become more comfortable with presence, you might try experimenting with your attention. See if you can allow your attention to expand beyond your body. Let it widen to include the space around you, the space within which all you perceive is appearing. Now see if you can perceive *from* that space. See if you can *be* that space. Let go of everything and rest as that pure space of awareness.

As always, take care of yourself. Don't push yourself too hard. If you're having difficulty, stop and check in with yourself: "What do I need, right now? What do I need lifted? What do I need freed?" As I've said, asking is powerful. In simply offering these questions into the space of awareness, there is automatically a receiving that happens—not necessarily of the answer, but of a subtler, more direct communication from *being* itself.

Importantly, don't be too serious. Be playful with yourself if you can. Many people approach spiritual practice with a kind of somberness or over-seriousness. So if "spiritual practice" sounds weighty and serious to you, drop that whole idea—and call it something else! See if you can come up with a different description of how you're spending all this time—ideally a funny one!

Don't try too hard to control your mind. If your mind has been torturing you, maybe dive in and see if you can get it to entertain you instead. Work on your fantasies. Embellish your illusions. Massage that mind! Don't try to force it into a narrow, rigid little room if it doesn't want to go there. Instead, give it the universe. It's that big; in fact, it's bigger.

I know what I'm offering here is a little different from the usual meditation advice! But it's important to be flexible, to not limit yourself. Most people find it helps to allow a bit of freedom into their meditation practice. Say your mind is wandering incessantly and you're finding it impossible to stay present. Instead of beating yourself up about it—"I'm so distracted; I can't pay attention; I'm a terrible meditator"—drop all that and just go with it. Don't fight it! Let your mind wander, see where it goes.

Give your mind some space, some room to do what it does. Is it jumping off into fantasy? Let it! Go ahead and have a fantasy, and when the fantasy has run its course, come on back and see what's going on right here, right now. How does your body feel now? What changed? What didn't? Maybe you'll learn more about yourself this way than if you'd stayed "focused." Maybe you'll gain more insight into what's underneath that impulse to fantasize if you allow it to move, and even blossom a bit.

If you restrict yourself too much, even for a so-called "good reason" like "meditating correctly," you create a kind of contraction. You strengthen the *identity* of the one who wants to get enlightened, the one who wants to be free of suffering. If you give yourself more permission, more room to breathe, that's less likely to happen. You'll be much less caught, less invested in and identified with the hoped-for results of your efforts.

It's a bit like being a musician. There's a big difference between a musician who is *inspired* and one who is merely technically skilled. Their performance, their expression, and even their body language are very different, much more relaxed and free-flowing. This is also true of someone who is *alive* in freedom, who is available to the movement of transformation.

This is an element that's often lacking in very disciplined training. The point of that kind of training is to learn the techniques, to attain a certain proficiency and a kind of mastery in them. But becoming a highly skilled meditator by no means guarantees you'll find freedom. Sometimes that kind of refinement can even become an impediment.

Often people who've been on really intensive practice regimens for a long time need to take a step back from that discipline and allow themselves some space to explore and be creative. They may need to question their practice and explore different perspectives about it—maybe even let themselves badmouth it and find it ridiculous! I love when people tell me they're sick and tired of their meditation practice and they feel like it's all been a big waste of time. My response? "That's progress!"

Sometimes when speaking publicly, I joke that people are probably thinking, *I'm sick of these spiritual events; how many more of these things do I have to come to?* Everyone always laughs! Every time. Why? Because at some point, on some level, everyone really does feel that way. The part of you that has those feelings needs to be allowed as well. Those feelings are real! Even if they don't seem like appropriately "spiritual" feelings, they're what's *actually happening.*

Along the way, you may find yourself opening and closing, moving in and out of the experience of presence. This is fine, and to be expected. Often when someone has had a taste of presence, or even an awakening experience or spiritual breakthrough, they're alarmed and disappointed when that awareness seems to recede again. This can be frustrating—you had a taste of freedom, and it seemed so permanent, but now you're back in the struggle. You thought you had it, but now you seem to have lost it.

But you can't lose it. You had it already; you've *always* had it. Gradually you'll find that these movements in and out of awareness no longer bother you. You may even find yourself resting as a deeper awareness that is aware even of moving in and out of awareness. But wherever you are experientially in any given moment, you'll find that you're okay with it. A kind of spiritual maturity emerges that allows you to trust your own process, and allows it to move as it will.

◇◇◇◇

Back in the monastery, I rarely did what they told me to do. On the outside it looked like I did—I showed up on time; I sat there; I bowed and chanted when I was supposed to—but internally I was definitely not sticking with the program. When we were chanting and bowing after *zazen*, I thought of it as singing and doing yoga. I didn't learn all the Japanese words and what they meant; I just enjoyed the singing. That was how I made it work for me.

So make it work for you. In whatever way you can, let yourself *be here*, right now, and keep being here. *Being here* is all that's required, regardless of how "successful" your practice feels at any given point. At times you'll find yourself going with your experience and letting it happen, while at others you'll find yourself resisting, fighting, making it more difficult. At still other times, you'll feel neutral, flat, a bit blasé about it all. But *being here* works anyway because it isn't our effort that frees us.

What does free us is just this mysterious, unknowable life force. We can call it presence, awareness, the Divine, or God, but labels are limited. Ultimately we're talking about the unknowable. So trust the unknowable. Be receptive and attentive to where you might be in the way. Be mindful. Be heartful. Be gentle, sensitive, and patient with yourself. Take a bigger perspective.

42.

The Rude Awakening

Awakening to the truth is only the first step. After that initial awakening comes what I often call the *rude awakening*. The dark side—that which we've kept covered up, that which we've repressed—comes to the foreground. The light of awakening illuminates the darkness, making visible what has been hidden, the parts of ourselves we haven't wanted to see. This can be quite disturbing at first, but it is the necessary beginning of the journey to healing and integration.

Within most people there's a lot of unconscious and sometimes traumatic material that's gone unseen. When you begin to open spiritually, the light of awakening is very bright, but that shadow is also enormous and powerful, and can become much more visible in ways you don't expect. As you open more, you suddenly realize that who you actually are is much bigger than who you thought you were.

Now there's much more space in your being. Because there's more space, that which has been stuffed in the closet or crammed in a corner finally has room to move and emerges from the cage where you've hidden it. What has been unconscious—whether repressed, ignored, or just never noticed—suddenly becomes conscious.

This can be very challenging. Often we begin the spiritual path to get away from just that kind of thing, right? But it's how the process works. You just have to hang in there, with compassion, forgiveness, and patience with your human self that's just trying to survive and be comfortable. This is where it's important to allow yourself some softness, some tenderness, some gentle loving kindness. Ease up the screws. Give yourself the space and permission you need to go through whatever you need to.

This is also where having a good body-oriented practice that facilitates grounding is very, very helpful. Expression is also essential. Expressing or voicing the truth of the condition can help that energy move and flow through and out of your body as healthily as possible.

As always, it's important to continually tune in to your experience and be aware of how you're operating. Notice where you're getting in your own way or holding back expansion. By holding back, you may avoid feeling uncomfortable temporarily, but ultimately that energy will move, with or without your cooperation.

An initial awakening can be a very enjoyable experience. That openness, that sense of freedom, is a great relief. So when difficult material like this suddenly begins to emerge, many people lose faith. You thought you were free, but now you're back in the struggle, right? You may feel like you've gone backward, or that you've lost something, or done something wrong.

I have one thing to say: Don't worry! These kinds of developments are not only fine, but entirely to be expected, and are even signs that you're on the right track. This transition can be difficult, but gradually you'll learn how to pay attention to what's happening, how to express it, and how to really feel it. As you become able to truly allow that difficult material to emerge in to awareness, it will actually deepen and strengthen your awakening.

Awakening is a radical change in perspective, and I don't just mean it will give you a better attitude. Who you are and where you're coming from will radically transform. The simplest way to describe it is *profound acceptance*. Acceptance is not an attitude or an intellectual or even emotional perspective. True acceptance is possible only from the space of awareness.

That's why I emphasize *being awareness*. As your identity shifts from your limited personal human identity to awareness itself, you finally have the space for that acceptance. Now you can really open to the broken or traumatized parts of yourself and allow them simply to be as they are. Whether or not those parts do heal or transform is secondary. You've taken away that pressure. You no longer have that expectation. Ironically, when you let go of the need for healing to happen, things often change in ways you wouldn't expect.

I'm not saying you shouldn't also explore other methods for addressing these kinds of issues, by the way. Formal mindfulness practice, therapy, various kinds of trauma work—all of these can be very helpful at the right time and with the right framing. As always, explore! Experiment. Find out what works for you.

But I think the most powerful approach is simply to be with *what is*, as it is, from the perspective of your true self. You won't necessarily heal right away, but by allowing deeply, you set the stage for healing to happen.

◇◇◇◇

The more I tune in to my body, the more I realize I've spent a lifetime avoiding it. Now the more I open up, the more pain I realize I've kept down and will have to experience now. That prospect is so scary that I find myself shutting down again, wanting to disconnect completely.

I understand. Fear is an intense emotion, maybe the most intense of all emotions. It can feel like it's just too much, that it will overwhelm you.

When you're faced with that kind of energy, that kind of intensity, the first thing to do is get yourself grounded. Sit so that your feet are flat on the ground, and place your hands on your legs. That will help your body be a better channel for all that energy. Feel your hands on your legs, feel your legs on the chair, and feel your breath moving in, moving out. Let your body settle.

Fear is often an indicator that opening wants to happen, so bringing awareness to the fear may reveal what's underneath it, wanting to emerge. A lot can be stored in the nervous system, but as we learn to relax and allow, all will transform, brighten, and expand. It could be a bumpy road, but that's why Rumi said,

> *You should wish to have a hundred thousand sets*
> *of moth wings, so you could burn them away, one set a night.*

It's all fuel for the fire. All these conditions are just parts of us that need to be reclaimed, reintegrated back into essence.

◇◇◇◇

I want to emphasize yet again that awakening is not a location or accomplishment. Awakening is ongoing. It's literally *what we are* in our essence. You don't *get* balanced; you *are* balancing. You don't awaken; you *are* awakening. You don't *get* healed; you *are* healing. Along the path there will be very, very pleasant experiences and probably some less pleasant experiences as well—some difficult, cathartic movements.

As the process deepens, though, you'll find that *whatever* is happening, it just gets better and better. I'm not saying you'll get to a point where you have no problems on a human level—that you'll never have health issues, relationship problems, or financial difficulties again. There will always be things in life that are challenging and difficult, but *how* you relate to and experience those things will be completely transformed.

43.

Being Is the Fullness of Life

Whatever's happening right now is, in its essence, perfect. Of course our mind doesn't believe that and usually has a story about some other set of circumstances that *would* be perfect, that would be preferable. But *being* is free of that story.

Being is the fullness of life—right here, right now. Not later! So why are we running around trying to get it? Because that's how the survival-oriented personal self operates. It does things. It grasps, it gets. And actually, that's fine! It's fine for the self to do its thing, so long as you're not identified with that doing. That's an important distinction to make. When you're simply being awareness, then doing can happen by itself.

Everything is allowed. Everything is welcomed. Even resistance! Does that mean you should like resistance or approve of it? No! It simply means that resistance arises, moves, and passes away within this spacious awareness that is your true nature, that is what you are fundamentally. So be the awareness that perceives whatever is happening, and you will be sowing the seeds of liberation.

The light that we are wants to shine; it wants to expand. That's its nature. All that's preventing it is our attachment to our suffering. Preventing that expansion is the very nature of suffering. So we only need to find out *how* it's being prevented and give attention to *that*. We don't need to change it, or fix it, or figure it out, or even understand it. We only need to see our resistance for what it is. The resistance is always what's blocking the light, blocking the movement of fulfillment.

◇◇◇◇

I'm not living my life fully. I desperately want to find fulfillment in this life, but it's not happening for me. I feel this deep longing for that fulfillment to happen.

You may not realize it, but there's a very subtle form of resistance at play here. You're maintaining an *identity* as someone who is not living life fully—as *someone* who is unfulfilled. What if you just dropped that identity? What if you were *just here*, right now, without any ideas or beliefs about being fulfilled or unfulfilled?

What we usually don't see is that our very longing for things to be different alienates us from the direct experience of things as they actually are. We need to be able to allow our experience to be as it is—to *be* the awareness that perceives even our resistance to how things are, and to live *as* that awareness, even in the midst of unease, dissatisfaction, or resignation.

We may not necessarily like what's happening, but we can still welcome and acknowledge it in the space of awareness. When that welcoming finally happens, you'll find there *will* be a moment of fulfillment, of opening, a moment of peace or expansion or light. That moment will be your guide, the signpost that shows you the way.

Welcoming even unpleasant or unwanted experiences does require a great deal of sensitivity, and also tenderness and compassion toward this limited human organism that we are. Suffering is painful, and it's also obviously not conscious. We certainly don't suffer on purpose! So we need to take care not to blame and judge ourselves for our suffering.

The key to becoming liberated rather than identified is in recognizing where and what your various identities are. You don't need to change them or fix them. Any attempt to change them actually strengthens them, gives them energy—as does any attempt to reject them or transcend them in some "spiritual" way.

Often when people embark on the spiritual path, they feel like they can't be human anymore—that since they're "spiritual" now, they shouldn't have normal human experiences or normal human feelings. But that's a trap, just another limited identity, and actually one of the most difficult to see and let go of. When finally you let go of even the "spiritual" identity, you find that you experience and feel more deeply than ever before.

As you move into this much bigger realm, you also find true compassion for yourself. You may see that in your longing to be free, you've been too hard on yourself and pushed yourself in ways that were not healthy. But now that pushing drops away, your field opens up, and your being becomes radiant and vulnerable.

44.

Releasing the Struggle

I find that I'm deeply resistant and deeply shut down. It feels like all the doors are slamming shut, and I just can't see how anything could ever change. How can I create the space within me to allow those doors to open again?

This path is to embrace and allow *whatever* is happening, and when all the doors are slamming shut, *that's* what's happening—there's resistance, there's contraction. That's the reality of that moment. But what is it that *perceives* that resistance? What is it that actually *senses* that contraction? That which senses, that which notices, is itself the space you are seeking.

So it isn't that you shouldn't have the contraction. You don't need to get rid of it or fix it somehow. Instead, just take a gentle step back and redirect your attention to the space within which resistance and contraction are happening. Notice that you are aware of other things too—sounds, random thoughts, other sensations in your body. Notice that you can be aware of the contraction without it being the totality of your experience.

Now notice the feeling of *resistance to the resistance*—the subtler contraction of *not wanting* the resistance and contraction to be there. Bring your attention to that *not wanting*. And again, bring your attention to the space within which that *not wanting* is happening. Notice that you are not the contraction, and that you are also not the resistance to the contraction. Rather, you are that space that perceives them, the space within which they arise.

So you don't need to create space inside yourself. You only need to notice that space already exists. You're shifting your perspective from total enmeshment in the condition of suffering to the *awareness* of the condition instead—and then realizing that you *are* that awareness. You are the quiet space within which all conditions appear. This is not a denial of the condition, but rather a total embracing of it.

But I don't like it when I find myself resisting things I want or things that are good for me. I don't seem to have any control over it. I want to be free of all this.

Again, bring attention to your *not wanting* the resistance to be there. We often focus on the thing we don't want and overlook the more intimate dynamic of *not wanting*. I sometimes call that the *primary resistance*—the contraction of *not wanting* things to be how they are. If you can bring your attention to that *not wanting* and to the space within which that *not wanting* arises, I think you'll find things will shift for you in ways you might not expect.

The real key to awakening is becoming aware of your fundamental resistance to what is. When you really get that, you also get what's behind it. You get awareness. You get openness! You get the space you thought you were seeking, but now realize you had all along—the space you now see that you *were* all along.

In any moment, you can take that step back to the perspective of spacious awareness. That's not to say you adopt a pose of detachment; that would imply a separation from your experience. But here there is no separation. There is only embrace.

Holding yourself to some kind of spiritual ideal that says you shouldn't be having the experience you actually are having is not helpful. You can do yourself a lot of damage that way. It's important to be honest with yourself about where you're really at—to, as we used to say, "Tell it like it is." By acknowledging the reality of your condition, you offer that condition into awareness. In that offering, your being expands. Your sensitivity grows. Your spaciousness grows.

In giving everything to awareness, you find that it gives you everything as well.

So right now, in this moment, with love and with tenderness, really acknowledge the truth of where you *actually are*. Recognize and acknowledge how you're feeling, even if it's not how you wish you were feeling or how you think you should be feeling. This is not about judging yourself, or condemning yourself, or identifying problems or issues to look at later. This is about just being honest—about laying your cards on the table, and letting yourself be exactly as you are.

Our humanity—our flawed and limited human existence—is actually incredibly beautiful, even with all its challenges, pains, and imperfections. Our human selves deserve our compassion and appreciation for trying so hard to protect us and take care of us. So even if you're not feeling wonderful right now, try to give your limited, human self a little love, a little gratitude just for being here, for being your vehicle in this amazing human life.

I'm realizing a lot of my resistance is because I'm often overwhelmed by my emotions. I experience a lot of fear and anxiety. That's where I'd really like to create more space.

When you take a moment to pay attention—when you're actually able to be deeply conscious of what you're feeling—that consciousness is the space. You don't need to create space. Space is already here. You only need to let yourself move into that room that you didn't even know you had. Once you're there, you'll find you're seeing from a much wider perspective.

Take this experience of fear, for instance. Fear itself is just energy, a movement of emotion. Where I'd invite you to put your attention is on your *not wanting* the fear to be there—or on your *wanting* the fear to stop. As I said, people are often so focused on the content of their fear—whatever external thing it is that they're worrying about—that they overlook the *primary resistance* that is actually perpetuating the fear. In resisting the fear, you contract around it and actually keep it in place.

So see if you can bring attention to that *not wanting* and again, to the space in which both the fear and your reaction to the fear arise. See if you can rest in that space—rest *as* that space—and just let the fear be there. You may find that the fear changes, or moves, or even transforms into something else altogether. Whatever happens, you'll gradually recognize that the space you wanted has been here all along.

Now that there's more space, there's also less pressure. You can relax a bit, decompress a bit. Maybe you just cry because the pressure's off and the grief can come out. The fear can come out; the anger can come out; the anxiety can come out. Whatever you've been holding in can move now, can be released and dissolved in the space awareness creates.

As human beings, we're at our best when we're emotionally fluid. The movement of emotion should be a very natural and easy thing. Emotion is the natural weather system of the body, but we've been conditioned to repress it, to clamp down on that energy. But as we deepen in this process, as we become more and more integrated in awareness, gradually we learn to let that energy flow again. At first this may be difficult, but over time it becomes easier, and eventually it's simply your default setting.

45.

Turn Toward What's Difficult

We often interpret the arising of fear or anxiety as something negative that we need to avoid, get rid of, or at least try to understand. But sometimes fear is actually a signal that the heart is opening. What you interpret as anxiety may just be the body's initial experience of vulnerability as long-held tensions begin to release.

When that release happens, there may be catharsis, there may be tears, but if you stay with the process, you'll find that there's also a lightness and a sense of release as you open into a bigger space. So I invite you simply to stop—and to listen, watch, and feel. Allow yourself to be open-minded and open-hearted. In the space that stopping creates, you'll begin to find out that as often as not, the very thing you've been resisting is the key that will unlock the door to freedom.

In Zen they say, "Turn toward what's difficult." So the question, then, is *how* to turn toward what's difficult? Allowing ourselves to feel what's painful is not always easy and is also counter-instinctual. Our instinct is to shut down, numb out, and apply our favorite coping strategies so we can survive. But as conscious beings, we also have the opportunity—and the privilege!—to decide to simply sit quietly, to bring attention to what's arising moment-to-moment, and to notice the habitual ways our organism responds: how it processes and filters experience—and how that can change! With the application of simple attention, we find ourselves softening, becoming more available to our experience.

The other thing that helps is, of course, patience. For some of us, this is the most difficult thing. Many of us in this schedule-obsessed culture have built our lives around time, but in awakening we discover the timeless. We stop measuring how we're doing, how far we've gotten, how much we've accomplished. We stop wondering how much more suffering we're going to have to endure. Instead, we simply attend to that pain, that frustration, that impatience—right now, in this moment.

Each person is unique, but awakening is universal. It's the discovery of what you truly are and the deep understanding that *you are that*. Whatever you prefer to call it—God, the Tao, Buddha nature—you learn to allow it to take you. And it *will* take you—all the way home.

◇◇◇◇

My life feels like it's coming apart. It seems like everything is on the verge of falling to pieces, and I'm feeling immense fear. I've been having difficulty sleeping. I'm running out of energy, and I don't know if I can do it anymore.

Fear and anxiety can be very powerful, challenging waves to surf. It can be overwhelming to have that much energy going through the system, through the physical body. So let's start by helping you get a bit more grounded—by having you become more kinesthetically conscious rather than analytically conscious. I think that will give you a little bit more support.

So take a moment to just stop. Bring awareness to your feet on the ground, your legs on the chair, and your breath in the belly. Let yourself drop out of your head and into your body, into your heart. Tune in to what's actually happening, right here, in this moment. I think you'll find that something in you wants to move—some feeling, some emotion. It's like a bud that wants to break open, wants to bloom. But don't *try* to open it, don't dig into it, just notice it, sense it in your body in whatever way you're aware of it—physically, energetically.

Notice also if there's any anticipation. Sometimes fear and anticipation can feel very similar in the body. If there's trepidation about feeling, that can block the movement toward opening. And if there is anticipation or trepidation, that's okay! That's simply what's happening in this moment. So bring awareness to *that* movement. Don't try to fix it or get rid of it, just allow it to be there in the space of awareness.

All that's required is simply to be aware of what's *actually happening*, right now, in this moment. You don't need to judge it, or change it, or somehow make it better than it is. You only need to meet this moment as it actually presents itself. This may be challenging at first, but gradually you'll find a softening of your experience, a relaxation of what's been tense and held in, and ultimately what you thought was unbearable may be the beginning of a beautiful flowering.

So what I'd recommend for you is to explore being very, very still, without any tension, so what needs to open can open. Otherwise the energy may get deflected back into its previous holding pattern in the body, which is what leads to the discomfort you've been feeling, this angst of too much held-in energy. Explore deep, profound stillness, and I think things will start to open for you. It may not be a big explosion, at least not at first, but more of a gradual, gentle expansion. The stillness will help you feel less vulnerable, less afraid of what's been held in. It will give you the deep support you've been yearning for.

46.

Change, Loss, and Tenderness

*I recently broke up with my partner, and I'm grieving the loss of the rela-
tionship, the loss of the friendship. I feel like I want to cry for hours, days,
but it's just not happening. It's like the tears want to come, my eyes burn,
but the grief doesn't come out. I feel stuck and stifled.*

Maybe there's something blocking those feelings, some other
feeling you haven't yet allowed yourself to acknowledge. Something
you haven't yet allowed yourself to feel. Maybe what's really needing
to be felt is your anger over the entire situation.

Sometimes we've just learned not to allow grief. Something
stops it, some belief we've internalized that somehow grief is not
okay. If that's happening, you want to *notice* what's stopping the
grief. When that becomes conscious, the grief will naturally move
because the heart naturally releases grief.

We've learned to stop our feelings. But if you can, just take one
step back and *notice the stopping itself*; then that process, that impulse
to clamp down, can become conscious. The value of awareness is
that it *illuminates everything*. We can start to notice things that we
normally don't notice.

So try it. Stop where you are, right now, and notice what you're
feeling. It could be really subtle—a pattern of thoughts, a barely per-
ceptible contraction in the nervous system. Whatever it is, just allow
it to be there. Don't interfere with it, but also notice if there's anything else layered over the feeling itself—a compulsion to get rid of
the feeling, for instance, or even just a simple desire to understand it.

Especially notice any impulse to block the feeling or shut it down. Stay in awareness and observe very carefully.

I think you'll find that as you apply awareness in this way, a kind of insight will arise, and naturally your heart will begin to discharge the pain it's holding in. I don't mean intellectual insight, but rather simple, direct seeing of what is actually present. There's no need to analyze it or understand it. All you need is simply to see it. In that seeing, your heart will open, and your relationship to your pain will transform.

◇◇◇◇

I recently left my job and career. I'm very clear that it was the right thing to do, and I don't regret it, but even so I'm feeling a lot of loss and also some shame about it.

You've gone through a big transition, so naturally you're a little off-center. You're feeling a lot! So how is it *right now?* Take a moment just to tune in. Feel your body—your feet on the ground, your legs on the chair, hands on your legs, your breath moving in and out. Bring more awareness into the whole body. Relax if you can. Your body needs you right now, so really offer it some tenderness, some loving attention.

As your body relaxes, you'll see there's more emotion coming up as your heart releases what it's been holding in. When we're able truly to give ourselves love and compassion, our spirit rises, our heart opens, and we are naturally liberated from our pain.

Feel how you're connecting now. You're opening up, and as you keep opening, there's a lot more that will move. That grief, that loss, may be moving for a while, and you may even find it's just a reflection of something older and deeper in you that needs to move. So stay with that movement. Give it your gentle, compassionate attention, and let it do what it needs to do. Let yourself be fully human— fully present with what's actually happening for you, right now. Now your whole being opens up, and it is beautiful.

It's so important to bring this kind of tenderness to your limited, personal self. So many people focus mainly on the spiritual work and, paradoxically, only get more contracted in the process. But as I've said so often, once we really understand how to approach our human work, the spiritual work happens automatically. So bring what's truly happening for you on a human level and offer it into the space of awareness. And if it feels right, ask for guidance. If we open ourselves and ask truly, deeply, then we are shown. We are guided, one little step at a time.

47.

Be Right Here

Just be right here. Relax your body, relax your mind, and settle into this moment. Bring your attention once again to the awareness at the core of your experience that is already open, already relaxed, and profoundly receptive.

As you open more and more into that presence, you become more alive, more radiant, more vibrant, more energized. At the same time, though, the process can have some rough edges. As you drop in more and more deeply, the identity you've always taken yourself to be begins to unwind, begins to dissolve. This can be frightening to the mind, and if you're not gentle with yourself, it can also be rough on the body.

Fortunately, we have natural mechanisms that regulate transformation. So learn to trust those mechanisms. Trust your body when it tells you it can't handle any more; trust even your mind when it tells you you're at your limit. Self-care is very, very important on the spiritual path. When your body or mind tells you it's overwhelmed, back off and take a break. Don't push yourself.

Remember, you're not doing this. Rather, you're getting out of the way as best you can and allowing it to happen. You can plant the seed of transformation, but then you have to trust that it will sprout and grow, all by itself. That natural movement is no different than a blade of grass growing. You can't help the grass grow by pulling on it! You only need to nurture it and allow it to be what it already is.

You are here reading this right now because you are ready for it. You were drawn to this material because on the deepest level you understand that this process is already happening. It's growing, opening, and evolving you, transforming who you think you are. So let go of controlling, manipulating, and analyzing your experience. Drop your judgments and conclusions. Let go of knowing what's going on at all!

Of course your mind wants to know what's going on. As humans we all want to feel secure. We want to know we're doing it right and that we're on the right path, making the right decisions. But ultimately you have to relinquish the control of *knowing* and instead trust in a deeper kind of understanding—the natural guidance system that is the movement of our very life force. As you surrender more and more to that guidance, then naturally you let go of effort; you let go of pushing and trying. You let go even of trying to become enlightened.

That's not to say you abandon your human life and let it fall into disrepair. Not at all! You very much continue to take care of your life. You take care of business, you make decisions—and you learn! You continue to develop and grow as a human being. You explore and evolve on a personal level. You become more sensitive, more caring.

When I say you become more sensitive, I mean that quite literally. As you relinquish the control of *knowing*, you're no longer interpretively filtering your experience. You're letting a lot more in, and as a result you're now receiving a lot more information, a lot more input than you've ever been conscious of before. To truly allow *what is* to be as it is—to open to what is *actually real*—is to become open in ways you've never been open before.

People are often quite insensitive because they're so controlled, so *in* control. They're deeply enmeshed in *knowing*. They know what they think, they know what they believe, they know who they are— and so nothing touches them. Nothing *can* touch them. Their ability to receive input is very constrained, very narrow compared with someone who's wide open and available to receive. If you're truly opening, you can't *not* become more sensitive.

As you become more sensitive, you feel less and less separate from others, and so naturally you have more compassion. You empathize with others directly because you're not separate from them. Keeping people at arm's length is no longer even an option for you. When you're not as controlled, you're also not as identified with being a separate person, being a separate self. Identification is a kind of contraction, a tension. As you become less controlled, you become more relaxed, and the hold of identity naturally lessens as well. You can't be more sensitive or caring as a human being than when you are truly open, truly selfless.

◇◇◇◇

I've offered various practices and inquiries in this book, and there are of course many others out there for you to explore that can help calm your nervous system, heal the body and mind, and integrate your energy systems. As you deepen in awareness and begin to really let go, it helps to be as clear and balanced as possible so the energy can move—because it will definitely move! You want your body to be ready and able to accommodate that energy. If you put rocket fuel in a VW Beetle, it's going to have problems. That's why people have been doing these practices for so long—they really help!

So find out what works for you—how best to take care of yourself. Eventually you may get to a place where what works for you is nothing at all—just *being*. For now, though, continue to cultivate your awareness in whatever way does work for you, and pay close attention to whether what you are doing in any moment strengthens the separate self.

It's actually quite easy to know when that's happening—you can feel it. In any given moment you are either opening or closing, expanding or contracting. You are flowing and connected, or you're holding on, retreating into your fear, your longing, your grief, your rage.

So you meet yourself where you are, each moment, with tenderness and, ultimately, acceptance. That's all. You may not always like where you are, and that's okay! Gradually you'll be able to accept even that, and welcome it: "This is what I get to be with right now. These pains in my body, these feelings in my heart. This confusion in my mind. This is what's asking for my attention, right now." When you pay attention to what's happening, to exactly where you're really at, energy goes there, presence goes there.

This is a wonderful practice not only internally, but also in your relationships with others. Someone may be really pushing your buttons, seriously triggering you, and that reaction can itself be a teaching, calling you to ask yourself, "Do I want to have this tension in my throat, this holding in my heart? Is this how I want to live?"

If the answer is no, then instead of directing energy outside of you, toward the person who's triggered you, bring it back in and direct that awareness to the source of the tension, the source of that reaction. Now that triggering is an opportunity.

So the dark becomes the light; the reactivity becomes the movement into freedom. Gradually you understand, profoundly and viscerally, that everything—your thoughts, your feelings, your body—everything is fundamentally presence and energy.

So let awareness heal you. Let it heal your body and heal your heart. And don't rush it! Let it take all the time it needs. Actually though, there is no time. Awareness is timeless. There's only what's happening right here, right now. This appearance, this apparition. This dance, this love. This closeness.

48.

Life Begins with Awakening

Awakening—the direct experience of our true nature—may be just a brief glimpse at first, a little taste of infinity, or it may persist longer, as a kind of luscious steeping in awareness. Over time you may find yourself moving in and out of awareness, in and out of presence, probably many, many times. Over time, though, you'll find yourself settling more and more into this presence that you are—that we *all* are—and gradually it will become your resting place, your home ground of being.

There are so many different ways awakening can unfold. Prior to that initial glimpse, that first realization, explanations and translations may seem to be necessary. Models, road maps, and guides can all be very beneficial. But after realization, spiritual ideas, systems, and methods fall away. Explanations are no longer needed because now you see clearly that *everything* is mirroring the truth. Everything is teaching you. Everything is guiding you.

This realization—that this infinite awareness is what you fundamentally are—is the beginning, the middle, and the end of the path simultaneously. Now awareness and understanding shift radically. The truth is revealed, and everything changes. Your mind is relaxed, malleable, endlessly flexible. No longer caught in rigid habits of thinking, you're no longer enslaved by your beliefs, or anyone else's beliefs either. You're free of all that.

So now what? What's next? You don't know! From the awakened perspective, each moment is a new discovery. It's all brand new, always brand new, always *right now*. There's no anticipation, no expectation. There's just this radiant aliveness, this vibrancy of being, and a deep interconnectedness with all things.

It's fantastic to discover who you truly are, and the amazing thing is that this discovery keeps on happening, over and over. As one teacher of mine said when she was in her nineties, "I'm always learning new things and becoming more sensitive." That's the freshness, the innocence of pure consciousness—always learning new things and becoming more sensitive, and totally, totally okay with being human. I've often said that this path begins with awakening, but truly, *life* begins with awakening.

◇◇◇◇

Awakening brings you deep into the center of your humanity. Many people get involved in spirituality in the first place because they're tired of suffering and see the spiritual path as a kind of escape route. But from the awakened perspective, you now realize you don't escape at all. Rather, you arrive fully in your life for the first time. Now you *understand* suffering in an entirely different way. You can meet all the challenges of human life with a rich and complete engagement that's never been available to you before.

One of the biggest benefits is, of course, being free of the *need to know*. As I've said over and over throughout this book, living in *not knowing* is a great relief! The condition of *needing to know* is inherently insecure and deeply anxiety-inducing. When you find yourself no longer needing to know things so much—and for the most part, not worrying about *knowing* at all!—you'll see that a real shift has taken place.

When that shift happened for me—when the burden of needing to know finally lifted—it was such a relief! The experience of the shift was incredible—not only mentally, but also physically. As I said earlier, it was like a massive weight lifted off of my body. For quite some time I felt like I was floating, like my body had become literally weightless.

But of course experiences like that come and go. They can be very exciting and enjoyable, but in truth they're just signposts, markers along the way letting you know something is shifting. And then, gradually, the shift is integrated. You return to your ordinary human life, and although on the surface it may not look much different, your experience is completely transformed.

Presence is...always present! Always, 100 percent of the time. When you direct attention to it in a certain way, presence can become quite amplified, quite pronounced and foreground. But even when attention is more diffuse, even when you're tired or unfocused, awareness is always here. Always! The awareness of awareness, you might say, is constant, unbroken, ever present.

49.

You Can't Follow Anyone Else

Spiritual literature is full of different people's descriptions of their own paths. They may describe the awakening experience they had and the ways it transformed their experience—or offer a narrative or story of the steps they took along the way, an outline of their own spiritual journey. This is of course fine and often quite wonderful. Hearing other people's stories can be inspirational and motivating.

The problem is that when you hear about other people's experiences, you naturally find yourself comparing your own experience with theirs. "Why am I not experiencing that?" you may ask yourself. "What am I doing wrong?" You may then conclude that you need to do exactly what they did in order to have the same experience. That's an entirely natural and understandable conclusion to come to. But I want to tell you something very important:

It is not possible to follow another human being.

Each individual's path to freedom is completely unique. The essence of the path, this awareness that we are, is universal. But how it will heal specific people—what they'll experience, how they'll integrate it, the specific ways they'll be transformed—is a completely unique discovery in each individual human life.

So you can't really follow someone else. A good teacher helps you to find your *own* way and supports you in learning to simply live your own life, with all its challenges and pitfalls, while allowing you to deepen into the mystery and the insecurity of *not knowing*.

Naturally you want to get it right, you want to succeed, and that's fine for a while. But eventually that dynamic is recognized as a means of control, of holding on, of being somebody, and gradually you learn to let go of all that and simply rest as awareness itself. Awareness isn't holding on to anything, or being anyone, or being anything. Rather, it is *being everything.*

As your identity gradually dissolves into awareness itself—as you, in a sense, become the light—whatever is still held in is illuminated, revealed, energized, and ultimately disintegrated. This can be a very difficult, sometimes painful process, but eventually the attachment to getting it right—to *being* right—just isn't there anymore. At a certain point you begin to welcome being wrong! You realize that it's fun to make mistakes. It's fun to *not know.*

Surprise is a source of joy and aliveness. So allow yourself to explore and make mistakes, to be creative and not so careful. Instead of worrying about falling off the path, have the willingness to say, "I wonder what would happen if...?"

◇◇◇◇

As I've said, the most useful perspectives to have on the spiritual path are those of the explorer and the scientist. As an explorer, you are always wandering in unknown territory, always making discoveries. As a scientist you are constantly observing your experience and *questioning everything.*

I want to clarify that by "making discoveries," I don't mean "drawing conclusions." You're constantly discovering, but once again, you're not creating new beliefs. You may make new assumptions temporarily, but those can change at any moment. As you deepen on this path, your experience becomes fluid and free-flowing, and your thinking becomes much more flexible. Your mental and emotional processes become fluid, and your body becomes more relaxed.

Knowing that you can't follow someone else means accepting that you have to find your *own* way and embracing that ongoing discovery. The more you can be available to your experience in each moment, without trying to get something—even liberation itself!—the sooner that natural grace will bestow itself upon you.

You'll find out, more and more each moment, how this process works and how it wants you to participate. You might try one approach or practice for a day, a week, or even for years, and then find that, suddenly, it's time to drop that one and replace it with something else—or with nothing else! You'll see. You'll find your way.

Maps and pointers, models and schemas, can certainly be useful, particularly as you're getting started on the path, but eventually you leave all that behind. This isn't so much a conscious choice you make, but rather a natural moving on. You leave the map. You enter unknown territory. You recognize, finally, that you've *always* been in unknown territory.

It's amazing to see how many, many people are being brought to a place of awakening and to know that even awakening is only the beginning of the path. Awakening is the *beginning* of finding out how this life actually works—and that's great news! You finally get to find out how to be fully human. Your entire life begins to reorganize itself, and you find out how to surrender to *that* process and allow that realignment to happen. I've seen many, many people, including myself, go through that. It can take some time!

50.

Living from the Heart

After awakening, your spirit and your human nature are finally working in sync. You're no longer fragmented, no longer disconnected from yourself. As gradually you let go of the limited person you've mistakenly taken yourself to be, you finally become *fully* human. Now you're living from your heart.

To awaken is inherently to become more sensitive. That is, you *sense more*. You literally take in more information than you did before. You are no longer contracted, no longer protecting yourself from your experience by shutting down or by blocking it out, and so you are open and available in an entirely new way.

This also means you are much more aware of the energies and dynamics of your relationships with other people, and so your interactions with others take on a new depth. You see people more clearly, you feel them more deeply, and naturally you find a new level of compassion and tenderness for the people in your life.

This goes both ways in relationships—even as individuals, we're not closed systems. What affects you affects me, and vice versa. Even in an unenlightened sense, we're all affecting each other all the time. So as you open up and begin living from a deeper space, all the people with whom you interact will be affected, whether they realize it consciously or not.

From the awakened perspective, your whole view of "other" is completely different. Now you realize that there really aren't "others" in the most genuine sense, and even your sense of what interaction is shifts to a higher level. You relate to people more from the heart, from the big space of vastness and connection. In a way, you find that you're in love with everyone.

That's not to say you won't be assertive with people when needed or call them on their behavior when it's appropriate to do that. This isn't about adopting some airy-fairy "spiritual" point of view—in fact, you won't have a "point of view" at all. Rather, you will simply be open and available to *whatever* is happening and for whatever is needed. In that openness is the potential for a depth of understanding and compassion you've never had access to before. In a sense you will no longer *need* other people, but you will love them, deeply.

Being in love with everyone can be challenging in some ways, especially at first. You may need to relearn how to manage your personal boundaries and the ways you communicate with people. But at the same time, you now have the potential to communicate much more honestly and much more directly with all the people in your life.

◇◇◇◇

People often ask if their intimate relationships in particular will change after awakening. The answer is…probably! The truth is, I've never seen anyone pass through this transition without their personal relationships being affected in some very noticeable way.

You'll remember that earlier in the book I talked about energetic compatibility and how intimate relationships can really work only between people who are energetically compatible. Before awakening, though, it's still possible to remain in an unworkable relationship by shutting down emotionally and not really being honest or relating authentically to the other person. But after awakening, shutting down is no longer an option.

So if you're in an intimate relationship with someone with whom you are *not* energetically compatible, this will likely become *very* apparent after awakening, and that relationship will likely fall away. On the other hand, a relationship with someone you are energetically compatible with may shift as well, but in a direction of greater depth and greater intimacy.

You'll also find greater compassion for the other person's experience and point of view, as you're no longer so caught up in holding on to or defending your own positions. That's not to say you won't still have positions, opinions, and preferences; you probably will, and you may very well defend them at times. But you're no longer identified with them, and you'll find that you're more amenable to compromise and to really seeing and understanding the other person's perspective, which might be quite different from your own.

You may even find a new ability to go to the source of the relationship. What's the point of the relationship? What are you doing together in the first place? Often people lose touch with that. But now, from a place of clear seeing, you can see that purpose, and that makes it much easier to transcend many of the conflicts you may have on lower levels of interaction. You can move to a level where you both realize that what's really, primarily important is that you love each other and want to be together.

So you learn to listen, to truly be the space of listening within which the other person can express what they need to express and can have the experience they need to have. You can be present with your partner in a way you never could before. You have a completely different perspective—a perspective of pure attention, pure awareness, and pure loving compassion. It goes beyond the personal. It's the purest form of intimacy.

51.

Planting Seeds of Intention

When you're no longer identified with the personal self, you can plant seeds of intention in the vast intelligent awareness that we all share. In this way you align with the natural creative force of life, that living energy of creation and manifestation. We all have that ability; we all have access to that spacious awareness. From the space of deep listening, you just ask for what you want, and that request is received as it is offered.

Although this may sound like forming an intention and taking action to make it happen, this process actually doesn't involve human will at all. This "asking" is not an ego-based kind of request; rather it is something that is done *without* doing. When you're no longer caught in *being you*, what's left is simply the awareness of the mystery and movement of this life, and a very pristine sort of clarity arises. In that clarity you find a natural ability to envision a direction, a kind of path along which your life can move. As you rest in that connected field, you might find you just naturally inquire of that spacious awareness, into the infinite creative intelligence of life itself.

Because you're connected with that force—it's what we all fundamentally *are*—when you're open, you can align with that frequency, with that movement, and from that alignment you can, as it were, play whatever tune you like. You can ask for what you want or offer a certain intention. Or you can simply trust the movement and allow the movement to take you.

This is something that's difficult to talk about, another area where language is very limited. You might naturally want to ask, "If there's no will or ego functioning, why in the world would you even *want* to plant seeds of intention? From the perspective of awareness, aren't things already perfect as they are?"

When you are deeply tuned in and aligned, you might very well say something like "Everything is perfect," or "There are no problems." That perspective arises naturally from the connectedness of awakened consciousness—and it's true! But in that connectedness, you can also contribute to the process of creation, and you may just find yourself doing exactly that, without will, without effort.

From a more conventional religious perspective, this may sound a bit like traditional prayer, asking God for what you want, but it's not quite the same. You're not asking for something from a place of *needing* to have it or of expecting to get it. You may be asking for things to change in some way, but fundamentally you still accept reality as it is. Rather than needing change to happen, it's more that you have a profound willingness to receive, to allow that change in. You're aligning with the will of the life force itself rather than the will of your personal ego.

Now I'm very much *not* talking about the "new age" belief that we "create our own reality." That idea is usually a misunderstanding of this process, and most often does seem to be about "willing" your way to happiness, which I'm sorry to say just doesn't work. Worse, it can sometimes make people feel responsible for or blamed for their own misfortunes. Some people end up feeling, for instance, that by failing to be "spiritual" enough, they've caused their own problems. That kind of self-blame is the fast lane to the heart shutting down, which is why I emphasize forgiveness, compassion, patience, and an open mind instead.

The kind of creation I'm talking about is not willed at all, but arises naturally and without will, without effort. As you gradually settle into openness, resting in and living from your true nature as consciousness itself, what arises is a profound trust in and acceptance of *things as they are*—how they have unfolded in the past, how they are unfolding now, and how they will unfold in the future. There's a sense of commitment and even a certain responsibility, but without any kind of pressure, heaviness, or burden. Rather, there's a kind of tacit recognition that we're all creating this universe together, and also that creation arises from a movement that is much bigger than us, but that we are intimately one with.

My experience is that as you begin to explore planting seeds of intention, things come together that you could never, ever have planned, figured out, organized, or orchestrated. Doors open, things happen. People and opportunities appear. That's not to say you'll get exactly what you wanted in just the way you think you should get it, or even that you'll "get" anything at all. Rather, you'll find yourself trusting the movement of forces that are beyond you and flowing naturally with those forces.

By the time you're really connected deeply in awareness, you're comfortable with that connection to what we call the mystery, and you plant seeds of intention...*without* intention! Planting seeds is just part of your nature. You ask without asking. You inquire into the mystery because you *are* the mystery. You ask, offer, give, and receive simultaneously, and it's amazing what opens up when you do.

52.

The Meaning and Purpose of Our Lives

How is life meaningful when it can end at any moment? At what point does it become meaningful? When you've accomplished what you think you're supposed to accomplish? When you fulfill your goals?

Many people feel their lives lack meaning and purpose and that they have to find that meaning, or find their purpose. Some people identify what they think is their purpose and suffer when circumstances prevent them from pursuing it. "If only I had more time," they say to themselves. "If only I had more money…" Or they may feel deficient in some way and feel their personal issues are preventing them from succeeding: "If only I had more drive…" "If only I was more emotionally healthy…"

Other people go out and successfully achieve their goals, get everything they thought they wanted, and find they're *still* not happy and can't understand why. Despite their apparent success, something is missing; something is unfulfilled. They're still coming from a place of struggle and achievement, an energy that is inherently about grasping and attaining and is therefore impossible to satisfy.

The true meaning and purpose of life is to be at peace, to be fulfilled—to be happy! It's really that simple. That can happen for you regardless of your circumstances, regardless of whether you've gotten everything you wanted in this life or achieved all the so-called goals you set for yourself.

Goals and achievements either happen or they don't. There's no guarantee either way. What *is* guaranteed is that you can be free of goals, free of success or failure, regardless of what you choose to do with your life on a practical level. You may still have goals, and if you do, you'll still be more or less successful at achieving them at different times. The difference is that now your *identity* is no longer wrapped up in those achievements. You no longer need those accomplishments to supply your life with meaning.

Remember: This existence is like a bubble in a stream—at any moment it can pop. The purpose of life is to *live it fully* as much as possible, every moment. Not just when you're getting what you want, but also when you're *not* getting what you want, and even when you're getting what you *don't* want. Even when things are not necessarily easy, when circumstances seem quite adversarial, you can still live life fully. You can still be deeply, completely engaged.

From the awakened perspective, life is its own meaning, its own purpose. You become one with the life force, fully present and available for *whatever* is in front of you. Does that mean every single minute is going to be peaceful, or even look happy? Probably not! You're still a human being. You will still have challenges, but the way you meet those challenges will be transformed. The real beauty of this process is that transformation continues, endlessly.

As I've repeated throughout this book, awakening is not an endpoint. It's ever evolving, changing all the time. Now in my early sixties, I feel like I'm growing more as a human being than ever before. It's fabulous!

To awaken is to be fulfilled, to be happy, to be *alive*, free to live fully in each and every moment. I wish for you that fullness, that happiness, and that freedom.

The Beginning of Life

The power of *being* is incomprehensible. It seems so simple—just sitting here, resting in stillness. *Being* stillness. Being openness. Being this deep listening. The listener has dropped away, and now there's *just listening*. There's just being—and a continual discovery and profound healing in each moment. The idea called "myself," which we used to believe in so strongly, has fallen away. And now, finally, we truly come to life.

This is the real beginning of life—when we are finally *fully alive*. Now there's no resistance and no holding back—just complete surrender to this moment. In surrender, the truth becomes self-evident. No longer just a belief or a comforting concept, the truth is this presence, this radiant energy, this brilliant force of nature. We *are* this truth, healing and transforming everything.

I often repeat the instruction Jean Klein offered to me:

Just be this energy; don't think about it.
Eventually, it will be permanent.

The shift into being energy—being presence—happens over and over and over again. Now life is an experience of constant awe, one surprise after another. You never know what's going to happen. If you ever catch yourself thinking you do know what's going to happen, stop and look more carefully! Notice the filter that you're projecting through, the thought or belief that you know what's going to happen. As you see that belief for what it is, it drops away. Now, again, you see what's *really* here.

Our judgments, conclusions, and beliefs can hold back our energy and block it from moving. So keep bringing yourself back, keep noticing where you're struggling. That's where you're holding or blocking the energy. *That's* where to put your attention. The path is always *right here*—always right here in front of you.

Every moment is the beginning of this journey—and there is no end! There's no destination, no finish line, no endpoint to get to. There's only *here*. Only now. Only this closeness, the intimacy of this moment—this deep connection with the movement of being.

The movement of being is a natural, mysterious process, and gradually you learn to *let it move* in the direction it's moving. You step out of the way. You let go of control. You let go of *knowing*. You let go of believing.

There's really nothing you *need* to know. There's no action you need to take. You only need to *allow* the veil of illusion to be seen through. This awareness that we are this radiant presence is the very light of transformation. It guides us, and heals us, and transforms us. It is the essential energy of this miraculous life force that we are, and gradually we learn to trust it, deeply.

So relax into this moment. Drop the future. Drop the past. Feel yourself falling into openness right now, and give *that* your attention. Open to that openness, and gradually you'll find that it's here for you, all the time, without effort. Without thought. Balanced and open. Limitless.

Jon Bernie is a contemporary spiritual teacher whose teaching focuses on returning attention to the already enlightened state that lies at the core of our human experience. He has four decades of experience in the Zen, Theravada Buddhist, and Advaita traditions, and was formally asked to teach by Adyashanti in 2002. Bernie is also an experienced healer and teacher of somatic embodiment, with training in the Alexander Technique, Zero Balancing, and Qigong. He leads classes and retreats in the San Francisco Bay Area and beyond, and does intensive, one-on-one work with individuals to facilitate consciousness development and deep emotional healing.

Foreword writer **Adyashanti** is an American-born spiritual teacher devoted to serving the awakening of all beings. His teachings are an open invitation to stop, inquire, and recognize what is true and liberating at the core of all existence. Adyashanti is author of *The Way of Liberation, Falling into Grace, Emptiness Dancing, True Meditation,* and *The End of Your World.* Based in California, he lives with his wife, Mukti, and teaches throughout North America and Europe, offering satsangs, weekend intensives, silent retreats, and a live Internet radio broadcast.

MORE BOOKS from NON-DUALITY PRESS

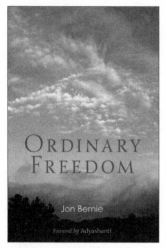

ISBN: 978-0956309198 | US $14.95

ISBN: 978-1908664396 | US $16.95

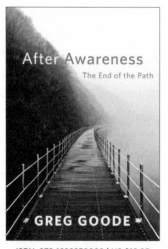

ISBN: 978-1626258099 | US $16.95

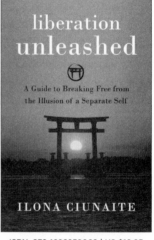

ISBN: 978-1626258068 | US $16.95

NON-DUALITY PRESS
An Imprint of New Harbinger Publications
www.newharbinger.com